'Effective leadership is more important in the complex and fast-paced world of today than ever before and the need for accessible and tried-and-tested approaches to enhancing leadership has never been greater. This terrific book is packed with useful information, insights, approaches and tips derived from the author's extensive experience, knowledge and expertise. Regardless of whether you are a leader, an aspiring leader or are involved in developing the leadership skills of others, this gem of a book will give you a clear, comprehensive and highly accessible guide that will enhance your knowledge, confidence and skill. It is definitely one to add to your library.'

Sarah Corrie, *Professor, University of Suffolk, Ipswich; Founder and Director of Inspiring Transformation Ltd*

I0130535

'Kate's ability to distil complex psychological principles into practical, actionable strategies is one of the most impactful aspects of her approach. Her focus on neurobiology, communication through "ego states", and understanding human adaptation to change has provided me over the years with a robust foundation for tackling leadership challenges. These methods have not only enhanced my own leadership effectiveness but also empowered my teams to thrive in dynamic and often fast-paced environments. One of the standout aspects of Kate's work is her emphasis on psychological methods that are evidence-based and simple to apply. Her teachings explain the complexities of human behaviour, enabling leaders to gain deep understanding, drive performance, and maintain resilience.

I have personally experienced the transformative impact of these tools, allowing me to navigate high-pressure situations with composure and inspire others to perform at their best. Kate's emphasis on adaptability and emotional intelligence has been instrumental in my ability to lead through significant change. Her models have given me the confidence to not only manage transitions effectively but also support my team members as they navigate uncertainty.

This has resulted in stronger relationships, increased engagement, and higher levels of collaboration across the board. Beyond her methodologies, Kate's passion for empowering leaders shines through. Her ability to connect on a human level and provide practical guidance has left a lasting impression on me. The principles outlined in her book serve as an essential guide for anyone looking to elevate their leadership capabilities.'

Mike Grimes, *Customer and Planning Director, Manchester Airport Group*

'This book is a *must have* manual for the bookshelf of any leader. The models and advice within are simple to understand – but highly effective and useful in any workplace. I have been following Kate's wisdom and counsel on leadership for a long time. You won't find better than what is within the pages of this book.'

Nina Williams, *Global Director of People and Culture*

'A must-have resource for aspiring and established leaders. This book seamlessly blends psychological insights with evidence-based strategies to inspire authentic and effective leadership. Packed with practical and actionable advice, it's a powerful tool for leadership growth and success.'

Niki McKenna, *Headteacher, Luminate Education Group*

'Like spending time with a great coach, this book unpacks leadership through cutting-edge neuroscience and psychology. With practical reflections, insights on resilience, navigating change, and even how to handle your most challenging colleague, it's essential reading for today's people leaders.'

Gill Green, *Chartered Coaching and Clinical Psychologist*

'Kate's clear and concise overview of the three base models, especially the ego states, combined with examples that resonate with leaders allows a full understanding of the impact of this theory in teams and organisations. Use of the change curve to position the organisational context is genius.'

Duncan Pearse, *CEO, Northpoint*

'A must read for all new and experienced leaders. Kate clearly explains 'the why' we can feel so overwhelmed by day-to-day leadership challenges while giving practical, clearly articulated and easily implemented solutions. I can't recommend it enough if you want to bring together a high performing and cohesive team.'

Deborah Saffer, *Director of Information Security*

'As a leader in the charity sector I have applied the tools explained so accessibly and pragmatically in this book to better understand how to work as a senior team to become more than the sum of our parts.'

Sanj Srikanthan, *CEO, ShelterBox*

'Kate masterfully blends complex neuroscience with practical leadership insights, making this book immediately captivating. Visual models and self-reflection exercises guide readers through engaging chapters. Insightful references inspire further exploration, while the inclusion of transactional analysis and other frameworks empowers readers to navigate relationships and drive meaningful change.'

Tina Welch, *HR Director, GatenbySanderson*

'If you're seeking to take your leadership skills to the next level, look no further. Based on core psychological principles applied to different everyday leadership scenarios, you will learn how to speak in a way that ensures people listen to what you have to say. This book is the perfect companion for every leader who ever had responsibility for change management and, at some point, was faced with strong emotions or difficult behaviours from those they were leading. In other words, every leader will find this book useful!'

Sarah Brooks, *PhD, Lecturer in Organisational Behaviour and ICF accredited coach, University of Sheffield*

THE PSYCHOLOGY OF EFFECTIVE LEADERSHIP

Leaders are leading in unprecedented circumstances as the world of work is more complex than ever before. Leadership success can seem elusive. Simple, easy to follow and clear, this book takes complex and validated thinking and research from psychotherapies, psychology and neuroscience to create simple approaches that have been proven to work in helping leaders address the challenges and tensions experienced day to day.

Organisational leaders support their teams, driving performance and change. They are passionately committed to their organisation's cause and yet are often overwhelmed by what comes at them on a daily basis. This book explains how your brain works and needs to work in order to lead effectively. For example, it introduces the brain states of 'threat' and 'reward', what causes these at work and the likely and needed leadership behaviours to avoid 'threat' states. It presents the ego states, a model that allows us to understand and apply the mechanics of effective communication to leading, preventing conflict, misunderstanding, and, thus, increasing commitment and motivation. Tools and techniques are provided to influence and manage through change, increasing engagement and decreasing resistance.

This book is for leaders and aspiring leaders and those interested in the neuroscience of leadership. It is also for leadership development coaches, as it contains practical frameworks to use with clients answering the most asked leadership development questions.

Kate Pearlman-Shaw specialises in helping leaders to change their behaviours. She worked for 18 years as a UK Clinical Psychologist and leader, and has spent the past 20 years working internationally as a leadership development coach and facilitator for private and public sector organisations. She is a double Chartered Psychologist with the British Psychological Society, both as a Coaching Psychologist and a Clinical Psychologist.

THE PSYCHOLOGY OF EFFECTIVE LEADERSHIP

This Works

Kate Pearlman-Shaw

Routledge
Taylor & Francis Group

LONDON AND NEW YORK

Designed cover image: Rifqyhsn Design – Getty Images

First published 2026
by Routledge
4 Park Square, Milton Park, Abingdon, Oxon OX14 4RN

and by Routledge
605 Third Avenue, New York, NY 10158

Routledge is an imprint of the Taylor & Francis Group, an informa business

British Library Cataloguing-in-Publication Data
A catalogue record for this book is available from the British Library

ISBN: 978-1-041-03308-0 (hbk)
ISBN: 978-1-041-03310-3 (pbk)
ISBN: 978-1-003-62325-0 (ebk)

DOI: 10.4324/9781003623250

Typeset in Bembo
by Newgen Publishing UK

*To all those who have inspired me and, most of all,
to Jonathan and Mark, those I love most.*

CONTENTS

CONTENTS

ABOUT THE AUTHOR

Kate Pearlman-Shaw specialises in helping leaders to change their behaviours. She worked for 18 years as a UK clinical psychologist and leader, then, for the past 20 years as a leadership development coach and facilitator internationally for private and public sector organisations. She is a double chartered psychologist with the British Psychological Society, both as a coaching psychologist and a clinical psychologist. Kate has extensive experience running leadership development programmes, coaching teams and individuals where she uses the behavioural change skills and methods she learnt clinically in everyday workplace situations. She's facilitated hundreds of workshops and engaged in thousands of coaching sessions using those techniques that are drawn from psychology, neuroscience and leadership studies, enabling many leaders to overcome personal barriers and to change their behaviours in a range of key leadership situations.

PREFACE

About this book

This book is for leaders, any leader or aspiring leader, in any setting. This book uses well tested psychological methods that, in my experience, will help you to enhance your personal leadership effectiveness.

This book is also for leadership development coaches and professionals. It contains practical frameworks that have worked for my clients for you to use with your clients.

Why did I want to write this book?

The methods I use work. What you'll find in this book is a set of psychological methods that will really support you to enhance your, your colleagues', and/or your clients' leadership success. Years later, people with whom I have worked contact me asking that I take their own colleagues through the methods – because they worked for them. Apart from the materials I give or send out following the workshops or the coaching I run, you won't find these methods written down anywhere else all in one place.

This book is about leadership, the methods here will assist any leader, anyone who has responsibility for other people's work. This book will help you to get the best from those that you lead, and develop, and to do that without burning out.

Leaders are leading in unprecedented circumstances as the world of work is more complex than ever before. The leaders I meet are valiantly supporting their teams and driving performance; they are passionately committed to their organisation's cause and yet are often overwhelmed by what comes at them on a daily basis. I wanted to write something practical to help all of you who come to work with such positive intent yet struggle with the role of being a leader.

This book will ensure that these techniques and how they work in combination are widely available to anyone who wants them: leader or coach. You won't have to attend a workshop to understand and use them.

Who am I?

I am a psychologist through and through. I learnt to think psychologically when I trained as a clinical psychologist in the early 1980s. This way of thinking and seeing the world, quite differently from others, has stuck with me all these years.

I never expected to be where I am; I never expected to do anything other than work in clinical practice to support people whose well-being was challenged. As I worked my way up the leadership ladder, I found that the methods I used clinically worked equally well for managers and leaders. My journey into leadership studies began when I completed a leadership development course that I was subsequently asked to facilitate. Ever since then I've been helping people to adapt and change their behaviours and emotional state to become even more effective at what they do and how they do it. My approach relies on evidence based psychological methodologies drawn predominantly from the psychotherapies, neuroscience (as I started my professional journey working as a neuropsychologist) and the study of effective leadership, systems and change. I've worked with leaders across a range of sectors, countries and cultures. I keep being asked back. I keep being asked if these are written down in the way I present the psychology. They are now.

I've always striven to keep it simple: in clinical practice I had a sign behind my client's chair saying 'Work on the simplest thing first'. This too has carried forth: I am a 'conceptual translator',[1] I take complex methods and validated research creating simple approaches that work. It doesn't have to be hard to be your best.

Some of these methods come from my 18 years in clinical practice; some come from the following 20 years in leadership coaching and development. I learnt two of my three key models and how to use them in this straightforward and pared back way from my 11 incredible years with ORConsulting: it was Mark Hamlin who pioneered these methods, my colleagues and I refined them. Setting up my own consultancy in 2019 meant I have the freedom to add more tools for specific leadership challenges and formulate a package that I now use all the time.

What you get in this book is 40 years of my psychological experience, packed simply, of course.

How does this book work?

I use three key 'base' psychological models, I then apply them, with others, to a wide range of leadership challenges and dilemmas that my clients bring to me. I've modelled that process here: you'll find these methods in the first three chapters: first, leaders' neurobiology – how your brain works and needs to work in order to lead effectively. Then the ego states, a model that allows us to understand and apply the mechanics of effective communication to leading.

Third, the psychology of how humans adapt to change, the underpinnings of every leadership action from influencing someone to do something different to keeping them motivated and engaged. I recommend that you familiarise yourself with all three of these chapters before you tackle the rest.

In the following chapters, 4–16, you'll find the 14 'how to lead questions' that I am most regularly asked, that my workshops and coaching are most often about. These are grouped in the same order as the three base models, followed by a section that uses all the tools at once and a specific section on what's needed to be an effective twenty-first century leader. Once you've read the three base models, go to whichever leadership topic you are most interested in. These are written in the language of the base models, so having read these initial three chapters will make understanding what follows much easier. I end with my thoughts on today's leadership environment as I've seen so many changes to what's required to be an effective leader, especially since the pandemic.

Note

1 Term first used by Deborah Hougie. See Pearlman-Shaw, K. and Hougie, D. (2019).

Reference

Pearlman-Shaw, K. and Hougie, D. (2019). Is this a valid way to use neuropsychological insights? The art of, and justification for 'Conceptual Translation'. Paper presented to the British Psychological Society's International Conference of Coaching Psychology.

Section I

THE THREE BASE MODELS

1

MODEL 1

The neurobiology of leadership

This chapter introduces the reader to neurobiology, in particular the key brain functions that a leader needs to be aware of. As the brain operates in either a state of 'threat' or 'reward', these concepts are described in some detail as well as what causes these at work. The role of key neurotransmitter substances are introduced as there are four that are important to increase. Likely and needed leadership behaviours to avoid 'threat' states are introduced. The concepts introduced in this chapter will become familiar to the reader as the book progresses, as they are key to understanding how to lead even more effectively.

Knowing how your brain works and what you can do about it is a great place to start thinking about how to be an even more effective leader. Using recent discoveries from neuroscience to inform how we behave at work is of great interest in contemporary leadership studies, and to me. Since the advent of brain scanning in the last 25 years, we've learnt an enormous amount about how healthy brains work and now scientists are applying this to how humans behave in organisations and the implications for leadership.

When I started work as a basic grade clinical psychologist on a neuro-logical hospital ward, there were no brain scanner machines. We used pencil and paper tests to find out which bits of the brain were damaged after strokes or through dementia. We'd return to the office and leaf through 'Muriel', our text book by Muriel Lezak (1983) with all the correlations that would help us to be able to say where lesions were. Returning to neuroscience after 30 years has brought my career full circle. It's a subject I am com-fortable with, fascinated by and it's why I start my leadership development insights here.

Despite having 80 billion neurons in your brain and about 2.5 miles of 'wiring', of particular importance are two key brain regions:

1. *The cortex regions* behind our frontal lobe, the prefrontal cortex (PFC), deals with our complex thinking and logical decision making. It is our

DOI: 10.4324/9781003623250-2

integration centre. as pathways connecting most brain functions pass through, connecting here. The PFC is also thought of as providing 'higher executive functions' due to the coordinating role it provides. There are two accessible systems located here:

- The empathic network (or default mode network) which means the coordination, learning and thinking about our relationships. This is all about our 'relational knowing', includes our moral reasoning and supports our emotional regulation. This leads to reasoning involving intuition, empathy, interpersonal experiences and is linked to experiential learning
- The analytic network (or task positive network) which overseas our logical analysis, data processing, is responsible for planning. This is where we process anything complex such as understanding complicated situations, difficult decisions to be made or dense data to unpack. 'Slow' or 'deep' thinking is instigated here: this is the type of thinking that Daniel Kahneman (2012) identified in his seminal and Nobel prize winning book, *Thinking, Fast and Slow*

Commentators on leadership and neuroscience strongly suggest that we need our PFCs working and accessible in the workplace, especially for leaders whose role it is to be able to see the overview, think logically and join the dots as well as attend to relationships with colleagues and manage complex interpersonal situations. We need our PFCs to operate in modern day workplaces, often described as VUCA: volatile, uncertain, complex and ambiguous (US Army War College, 2022) or BANI: brittle, anxious, non-linear and incomprehensible environments (Cascio, 2020), as many of us do

2. *The limbic system* is a set of brain areas, including the thalamus, hypothalamus and the amygdala, that are our emotional and sensory reaction centres. These are connected to our sensory systems and are stimulated when we receive a pattern that matches anything we've found 'threatening' or disturbing in the past. When I trained, we thought there were five sets of sensory information feeding into the limbic system, sight, sound and so on. Now we think there are around 50: we receive sensory information from clusters of cells and numerous signals from all parts of our bodies, known as embodied responses. This is where our emotions are stimulated, including and most relevant here, our negative emotions, those we experience, and later interpret (in the PFC), as anger, fear or anxiety, sadness and loss and guilt and shame

When the limbic system is stimulated, it inhibits the effectiveness of the PFC. For some people this is a minor impairment, for others, the limbic system is

Pre-frontal Cortex

Integration Centre

The 'analytical' & 'empathic' system

System

Reaction & alarm centre (fight & flight)

Receives 50 sets of sensory data

Analytic:

Thinking
Logical reasoning
Understanding
Deciding
Evidence
Data

Empathic:
Emotional processing
Connection
Attachment
Empathy
Intuition

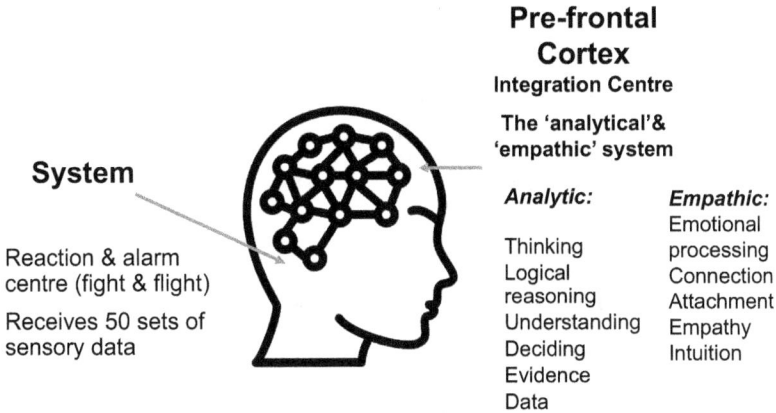

Figure 1.1 Depiction of basic neuroscience

thought to completely hijack the accessibility of the PFC. This means that logical, deep, evidential thinking is impaired; we are more likely to think automatically and illogically, to make 'thought errors' and become more biased. In addition, we construct the experience of those negative emotions. The combination of biased thought and heightened emotion means we are likely to experience behaviour changes, becoming less easy to get along with, perhaps more confrontational and less focused, none of which are helpful for effective leadership.

1.1 The role of hormones and the parasympathetic nervous system, the vagus nerve

The patterns described above are further compounded by our hormones. When the limbic system is activated, our dominant vagus nerve communicates with our adrenal areas in our abdomen, where adrenaline, cortisol and testosterone are secreted. These hormones add to the impact of the limbic system stimulation, making us go faster, be stronger and respond to threat. These we experience as stress. All of these were designed to protect us from threat, to provide our fight and flight mechanisms, yet, in leadership terms, this means our emotions, our thinking and our behaviour are impaired, where we are less likely to be able to lead effectively.

1.2 Threat and reward

The brain responds to social situations that we interpret, or have learnt to interpret, as threatening or rewarding. The brain behaves very differently in these two conditions:

In threat state decreased access to PFC

Pre-frontal Cortex
Integration Centre

The 'analytical'& 'empathic' networks

Limbic System
Reaction Centre
Highly stimulated

Analytic:
Complex Thinking
Logical reasoning
Understanding
Deciding
Evidence
Data

Empathic:
Emotional processing
Connection
Attachment
Empathy
Intuition

Stress hormones produced: cortisol, adrenaline and testosterone

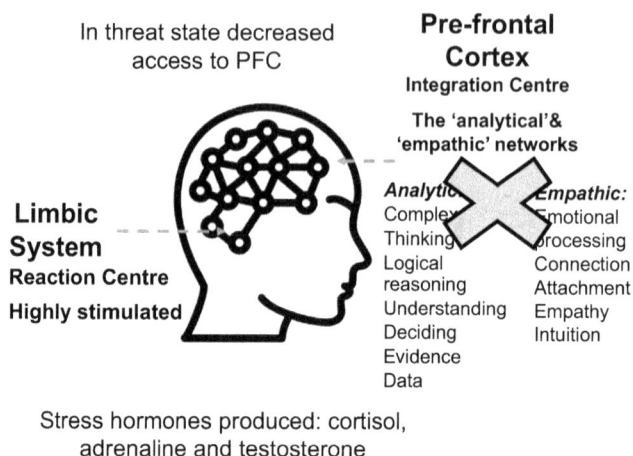

Figure 1.2 Depiction of threat state

- *Threat*: in social situations that we have learnt to interpret as threatening, the unsophisticated limbic system fires, making it harder to access, or even overriding, the cortex and our ability to think, thereby interfering with our higher processes – logical thought, decision making, social interaction and complex planning. The limbic system has hijacked our higher abilities and behaves as if a major life-threatening situation is happening. This is not when effective leadership occurs
- *Reward*: in situations we have learnt to interpret as rewarding, the limbic system is calm and not activated, allowing complex integration across our brain to occur. Under these conditions we can make and recall memories, more accurately perceive, use language effectively and are more able to learn. We can access deep and slow thinking. We can use our analytic network: we are logical, solutions-focused, decisive and realistic. We can access our empathic network, meaning we are more likely to be experiencing positive emotions and engaging more with what and who's around us. These parts of the brain need more time and energy to work properly and sometimes we have to work hard to engage it. This is the preferable state for effective leadership

Many studies have demonstrated that the brain operates to a key principle: it prefers to avoid threat and maximise reward. In fact, the brain is scanning for threat every five seconds and is also looking for situations to approach to gain reward.

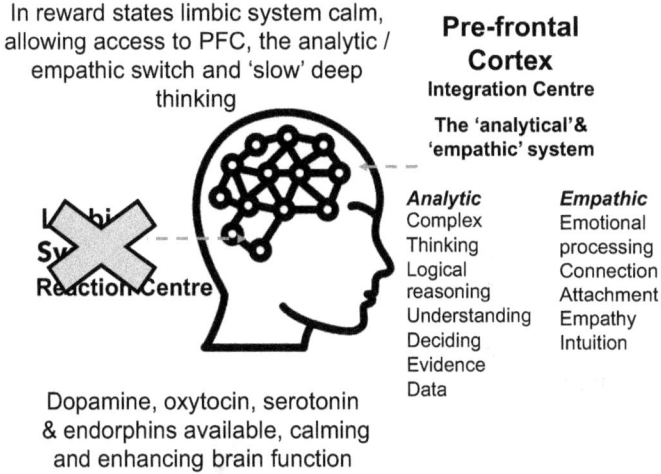

In reward states limbic system calm, allowing access to PFC, the analytic / empathic switch and 'slow' deep thinking

Pre-frontal Cortex
Integration Centre

The 'analytical'& 'empathic' system

Analytic	Empathic
Complex Thinking	Emotional processing
Logical reasoning	Connection Attachment
Understanding	Empathy
Deciding	Intuition
Evidence	
Data	

Limbic System Reaction Centre

Dopamine, oxytocin, serotonin & endorphins available, calming and enhancing brain function

Figure 1.3 Depiction of reward state

1.3 The role of neurotransmitter substances in reward

There are key neurotransmitter substances that help our brains to be in the reward state, sometimes called the 'renewal' state. These are oxytocin, dopamine, serotonin and endorphins.

Oxytocin is our bonding neurotransmitter substance. It is secreted whenever we have a positive interaction with another person (or our pets, or even ourselves). Previously thought to be secreted only in large amounts when women give birth, it's now understood to be secreted in smaller amounts through positive interactions with others. It's important as it subdues limbic system activity. Neuroscientists describe this oxytocin effect as 'bathing the limbic system in a warm bath'.

Dopamine is released when we are satisfied or rewarded. It allows us to feel motivated, pleasure and satisfaction. We don't want too much of this as very high levels are associated with poor mental health.

Serotonin has a key impact on our mood, impacting our happiness as well as helping our attention and our digestive system.

Endorphins are powerful opioids secreted through exercise and laughter. They are the body's natural pain relief and contribute to happiness, relieving stress.

We need to engage ourselves and others in actions to increase and maintain healthy levels of these neurotransmitters in order to gain and maintain 'reward' states.

1.4 Optimising reward states

There are a great many leadership actions we can do to stimulate reward states and more of these neurotransmitter substances:

- Listening
- Curiosity
- Understanding
- Compassion, empathy
- Honesty, transparency
- Inclusion
- Gratitude, thank you
- Recognition
- Being trusted
- Given information
- Able to decide
- Treated fairly

Interestingly, all these actions are considered highly effective leadership behaviours in contemporary leadership studies.

1.5 Leadership and the brain

Because the threat states are so detrimental, leadership authors suggest that we build rewards in organisations for increased effectiveness. The more we and our colleagues can reach the reward states the more effective we will be.

Everything in this book is based on this principle of threat and reward: every method that follows is to help you to get yourself out of threat and into reward and to do the same for those you lead and interact with.

1.6 Self-reflection

- Do you recognise threat and reward responses in yourself?
- Do you recognise threat and reward responses in those you lead and manage?
- What causes threat responses for you?
- What creates reward states for you?
- And what about that hard to lead person in your team: what creates threat and reward for them?

References

Cascio, J. (2020, 29 April). Facing the age of chaos. Medium. https://medium.com/@cascio/facing-the-age-of-chaos-b00687b1f51d

Kahneman, D. (2012). *Thinking, fast and slow*. Penguin.

Lezak, M.D. (1983). *Neuropsychological assessment* (2nd ed.). Oxford University Press.

US Army War College (2022, 6 December). Who first originated the term VUCA (volatility, uncertainty, complexity and ambiguity)? https://usawc.libanswers.com/faq/84869

2

MODEL 2

The mechanics of communication: the ego states

This base model is the one I keep being asked back to deliver. It's a simple model that explains why we communicate the way that we do, why we have the impact, often unintended, that we do, and crucially, how to make choices about how to communicate well. Known as the ego states, this model comes from a branch of Transactional Analysis (TA), which I think cleverly explains the mechanics of communication. It's really easy to use, containing only six concepts and words: you'll find you're able to understand, explain, and make choices about your own communication immediately after reading this chapter. Later in the book I'm going to address this model in more depth: Chapter 8 shows you the subtleties of using it and Chapter 9 demonstrates how to use this approach to manage difficult situations. You'll find the language of this model used throughout the book.

When we're in reward states we're able to communicate thoughtfully and effectively, whereas, in the threat states, our communication is likely to be more reactive, based on fight and flight. The ego states, or 'states of self', from TA, is a very pragmatic model of communication that demonstrates what happens in these two states. Significantly, this model also demonstrates the impact that we have on others, and gives us choices about how to alter our behaviour to have an even more effective impact. In other words, this is a model of the mechanics of communication that shows us what to do to stay out of threat and keep ourselves and others in a state of reward. It's highly visual and easy to pick up, helping us to make instant and lasting change. I've been told, and have seen, that it's completely changed some people's leadership style, and relationships at home.

2.1 Some introductory concepts about TA

Eric Berne, originally a psychoanalyst, started writing about TA in the 1960s as a way of making psychological therapies accessible to all. In his famous book, *Games People Play* (1977), his central concept was one of 'OK-ness' where everyone is born OK and events in life cause us to deviate from this

DOI: 10.4324/9781003623250-3

OK position, a concept later developed by the other well-known TA founder, Thomas Harris, in his book, *I'm OK, You're OK* (1969).

Important in the model are:

- Ego states are consistent patterns of thinking, feeling, and behaviour. Ego states are a central concept in TA: they are metaphors to understand our 'states of self', our internal, intrapsychic processes and relational patterns, otherwise considered our communication style
- Ego states are reciprocal and complementary. There are six ego states where each invites another ego state in return from another person. Three of these are thought of as effective, creating OK-ness in ourselves and others; in other words, creating reward states. The other three are considered ineffective, ultimately dysfunctional, turning people away from us, so creating and maintaining threat states
- The reciprocal nature of communication is important here: the law of reciprocal communication from social psychology tells us that every communication has a matching reciprocal response
- The model described here is from Organisational TA, a version developed especially for use in organisations in the 1980s by Abe Wagner (1981). There are more complex forms of TA that are mainly used in therapeutic settings that I consider unnecessarily complex for leadership development

2.2 The ego states

Although I will be focusing on six ego states, there are three overarching ego states to understand first: Child, Adult, Parent, and where each represents and communicates something different:

1. The Child ego state represents and communicates our feelings
2. The Adult ego state represents and communicates pure thinking, facts and logic
3. And the Parent ego state represents and communicates judgements, values and beliefs

2.2.1 The ego-states and reciprocity

One of the most powerful influences on our behaviour as human beings is the simple process of reciprocity. Each time we behave, we invite a response from other people. For example, if I shout at you, your likely responses would be to shout back or to stay quiet: these are fight and flight behaviours in response to a threat. Or, if you asked me a curious question, where I believed it was authentically offered, I am likely to offer an honest and comprehensive response. Gift giving is another example of reciprocity, if you give me a birthday card or gift, then my first reciprocal act would be to smile and thank you, later you'd be hoping that I will reciprocate and mark your birthday in kind.

The ego states categorise these reciprocal actions. Each of the three overarching ego states have matching reciprocal responses.

The *Child ego state* represents and communicates our feelings. When we are born the only form of communication available to us is to cry, or later smile, demonstrating our needs and emotions. It's named not because we are behaving in child-like ways, the child ego state represents this ability to communicate what we want and need, an ability we retain as we develop. When we communicate our needs openly, this invites more of the same and some empathy from others.

The *Adult ego state* represents and communicates pure thinking, facts and logic. As we develop, we acquire enormous amounts of information. This is the state in which we acquire and pass on that knowledge. When we ask questions for information or to communicate data and facts well, we receive information back in return.

The *Parent ego state* represents and communicates judgements, values and beliefs. As we gain life experience, we have opinions and are able to use our experiences to jump to conclusions. It is these judgments that we communicate to others, receiving two specific reciprocal responses back.

In TA, each ego state is characteristically depicted by three circles (see Figure 2.1).

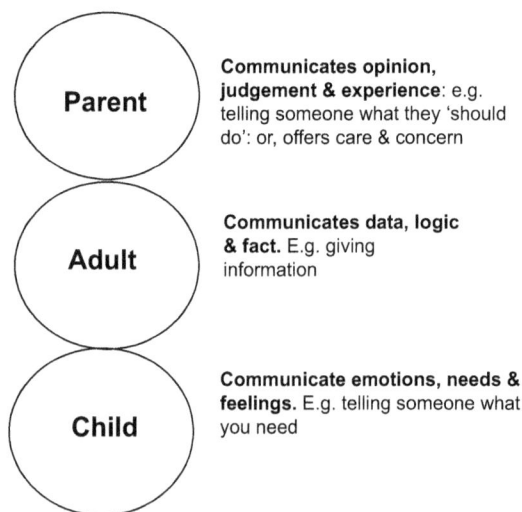

Parent — **Communicates opinion, judgement & experience**: e.g. telling someone what they 'should do': or, offers care & concern

Adult — **Communicates data, logic & fact.** E.g. giving information

Child — **Communicate emotions, needs & feelings.** E.g. telling someone what you need

Figure 2.1 The three overarching ego states

2.2.2 Introducing the six ego states

These three ego states divide into six:

1. The Child divides into Free Child as well as Rebellious Child and Compliant Child: all ways of communicating emotion and need
2. The Adult doesn't divide, communicating facts
3. The Parent divides into Critical Parent and Nurturing Parent each communicating different forms of judgement and opinion

Effective: three of the six are considered inherently effective in communication, they invite warm, collaborative, safe reciprocal responses from others, so increase OK-ness and 'reward' states where the PFC in the brain is accessible.

Ineffective: the remaining three ego states are considered 'ineffective' where we cannot be sure how others will respond to us, more likely to create 'I'm not OK' responses or 'threat' states, where there's some limbic system arousal.

In Figure 2.2, the three circles are now bisected into segments to create six ego states.

2.3 The Child ego state: the emotional behaviours

In TA, the Child ego states are about our emotions, the impact they have on us and how we behave when we are experiencing emotion. 'Child' doesn't signify age and it isn't about being childish. Emotions and the impact they have on us are as real for us as adults as they were for us as children.

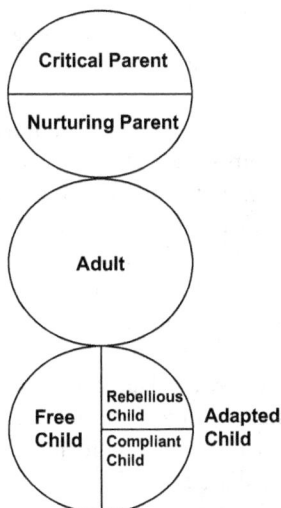

Figure 2.2 The six ego states

13

The Child ego state is divided into three different ego states where one is effective and two are thought to be ineffective. These three states are:

- Free Child
- Rebellious Child
- Compliant Child

Free Child: when we are in the Free Child ego state, we acknowledge our feelings to ourselves and to those around us. We recognise what we are really feeling and express this authentically to others. We are honest about how we feel, our wants and needs and our current situation. Our behaviour reflects this authenticity. We are able to talk about what is going on for ourselves and describe why we are doing what we are doing. This is also where we rely on our instincts and where we express creativity.

When we communicate from Free Child there are two likely reciprocal responses, or transactions: we receive honest responses back from others, or we are listened to and understood as we've invited a Nurturing Parent response (see Nurturing Parent, p.16).

Adapted Child: as we develop from childhood, we learn that it is not always smart to be open with our feelings; that, sometimes, it may be wise to keep our mouths shut and comply and, at other times, we are unable to contain our emotions and we fight back or rebel. Here we tend to adapt our feelings into behaviours and actions, known in TA as Adapted Child. Here we act out our emotions: rather than being honest and authentic we are unable, or not prepared, to explain how we feel. There are two positions the Adapted Child reverts to, either Compliant Child or Rebellious Child. Both are ineffective states as we are not being completely honest to ourselves or others, inviting judgement or scepticism from others. These are often highly reactive states, demonstrating a state of threat.

- *Compliant Child:* here we adapt our emotions into behaviours that are passive or even submissive. This is where we keep our mouths shut, comply and give way to others, for example apologise, give in or agree when we don't mean it. Especially in the face of domineering or aggressive people (perceived as threats), we find ourselves taking the path of least resistance and not being true to the way we really feel. This state is thought to reflect us responding in flight or freeze mode in response to stress
- *Rebellious Child*: here we adapt our emotions in the other direction, into behaviours that are defensive or even aggressive. We find ourselves behaving as if attack is the best form of defence. While we may feel hurt, angry or humiliated, our behaviours may be aggressive, defensive or resistant. These behaviours reflect the fight reaction to threat

Nurturing Parent Curiosity, Care, Concern & Collaboration Open questions with active listening, empathy, support, warm tone 'Us' and 'we' > individual	**Critical Parent** **Nurturing Parent**	**Critical Parent** I'm OK – You're Not OK Tell, poor listening Overcritical, judgemental Rules: "must, ought, should" Often loud with harsh tone. Aggressive or arrogant Manifestation of bias, all the 'isms'
Adult Communication, questions and conversation swapping data, logic & facts Analysis, problem solving Naming observations No emotion or judgement	**Adult**	**Rebellious Child** Defensive, push back, defiance Excuses, may lie, sulking Resistance, sarcasm At worst - sabotage
Free Child Open, honest self disclosure, authentic & self aware. creative, innovative, warm & friendly	**Free Child** / **Rebellious Child** / **Compliant Child**	**Compliant Child** False agreement, just getting on with it, submission Avoidant, passive

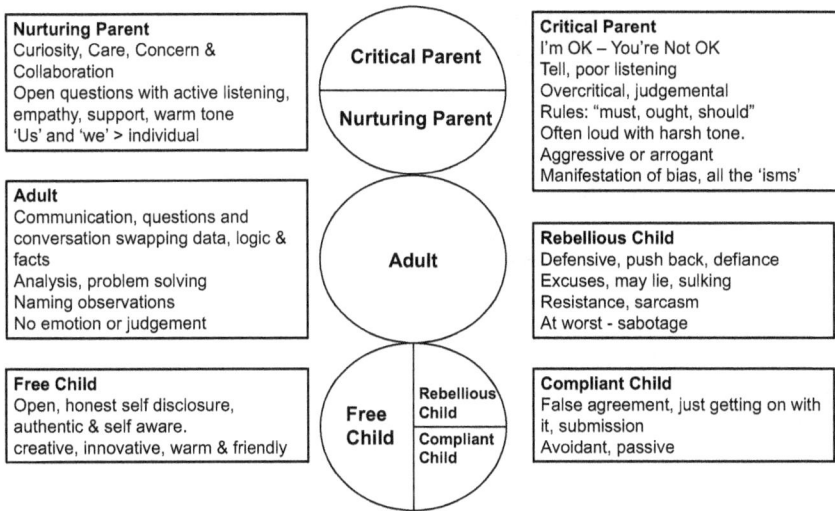

Figure 2.3 Communication from the six ego states

However, because Compliant Child behaviours are not reflecting what we are really feeling, we may eventually flip into Rebellious Child behaviour as we are really resentful or angry. For example, agreeing to something we don't actually agree with and then, later doing the opposite on purpose or taking it out on others around us. As we flip from Compliant Child to Rebellious Child, we may exhibit micro-behaviours and/or be seen as passive aggressive as small signs of those emotions become apparent.

Both these Adapted Child states are where we are not communicating at our best. These invite reciprocal responses of irritation, further defensiveness or avoidance and, crucially, we are more likely to be critically judged (see Critical Parent, p.16).

2.4 The Adult ego state: the rational behaviours

At other times we are primarily concerned with engaging our brain and operating at a more rational and logical level. Here we can engage the 'analytic network' that sits in the PFC. In TA, when we are focused on logic, facts, data, rational argument and debate, we are engaged in the Adult ego state. Similarly, we invite others to engage with us to focus on the data, by asking factual questions and engaging in fact-led dialogue, receiving similar reciprocal responses. When we are in the Adult ego state we are not demonstrating any emotion or judgement – this state only communicates and receives facts and information.

2.5 The Parent ego-state: the judging (or not judging) behaviours

As we grow up, we receive powerful repetitive messages from our parents or primary carers transmitting their own values and beliefs to us. In addition, we acquire a variety of life experiences that govern how we want and expect to live our lives. All these do's and don'ts, musts and oughts mean that we form a 'script' containing these rules, causing us to experience and judge the world as we do. This process of reaching judgements, here called the Parent ego state, is subdivided into two types, the Nurturing Parent and the Critical Parent.

Nurturing Parent is the part of us that behaves in a curious, empathic, respectful and supportive way. Fundamentally, the judgement here is that we trust the other person and agree with how they conduct themselves. This means that our first reaction to that person is to be trustful and open-minded. The Nurturing Parent style is to seek to understand first: this may be about where the other person is coming from and what it is that they need, or to seek context and reason for why something is happening. Nurturing Parent isn't about being 'fluffy' and all accepting, it's about truly understanding, seeking real insight into others and the wider world. Here we can access the PFC and activate the 'empathic network', which means we can behave in people-orientated ways.

When we are using our Nurturing Parent ego state, asking open, curious questions, listening with interest and showing warmth, the likely reciprocal responses are for someone to open up more, to feel safe and hear, to respond authentically, not hide things from us, as in Free Child. They are also more likely to use similar enquiring, warm, Nurturing Parent behaviours back.

Critical Parent is active at those times when we impose our judgements of what is right and proper on others and when we talk about what others 'should' or 'ought' to do as we see it. This is where we make negative judgements about other people. Critical Parent communication can take the form of judgemental, aggressive or controlling language and body language. It is often accompanied by a blaming tone, directed at the person directly: 'you shouldn't have done that'; 'you never listen'. Typical non-verbal behaviours include direct eye contact, faster language delivery and even a pointing finger. Critical Parent communications demonstrate that we are in threat states as we are not able to analyse or evidence check our responses, we are unguarded. Critical Parent is more likely to be where we demonstrate our biases, as these judgements are going unchecked.

Reciprocal responses to a Critical Parent ego state are the easiest to see. If someone judges you negatively or unfairly then it's natural to defend your position, or to get as far from them as possible. There's a very high chance that someone will respond to Critical Parent with Rebellious Child or Compliant Child adapted emotional responses.

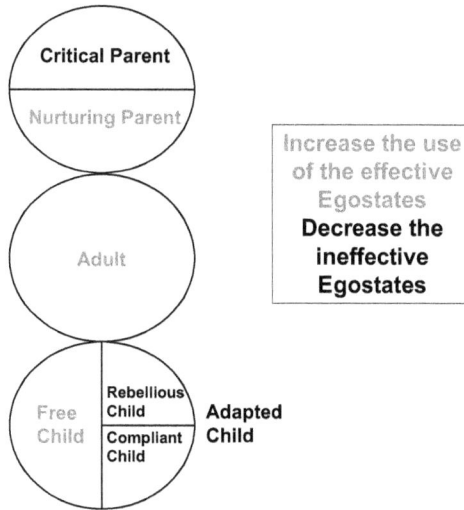

Figure 2.4 Effective and ineffective ego states

2.6 Effective and ineffective ego states

The term 'effective' simply means that you are using engaging, collaborative, authentic behaviours, making it more likely that you receive similar communication and actions in return. We are more likely to be in a reward state and be creating reward states for others. The ego states considered to be effective are Nurturing Parent, Free Child and, if there's no emotion or judgement, the Adult.

The ineffective ego states are considered to be Critical Parent, Rebellious Child and Compliant Child. It is true that ineffective communication choices can produce quick results. However, as consistent styles of interacting with people, the ineffective states soon give rise to resentment, irritation, demotivation or loss of credibility, all more likely to be perceived as threats to others.

2.7 Effective and ineffective reciprocity

Every time you interact with someone, you send out an invitation for them to reply.

Effective reciprocity. As a general rule, the effective ego states invite a response from other effective ego states. You will often find yourself doing this naturally, for example:

- If someone looks upset, you might ask how they feel (Nurturing Parent, inviting their Free Child)

17

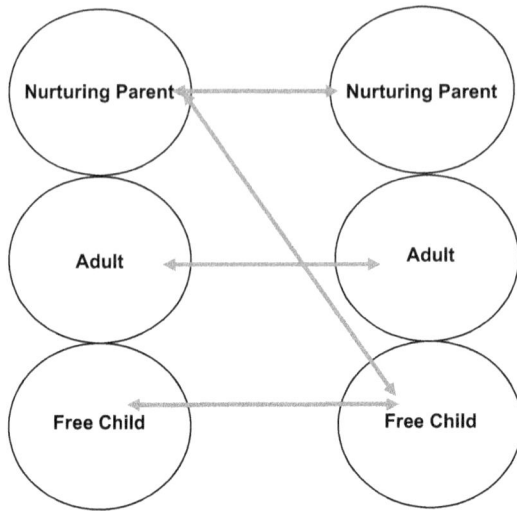

Figure 2.5 The most common effective reciprocal responses

- If you want to solve a problem, you may tell others what you know, and ask them their thoughts (Adult inviting Adult)
- If you want to lighten the mood, you may tell a joke or make a funny remark (Free Child invites Free Child)

This process plays out in every single interaction between two or more people. It works most of the time in most cultures.

Ineffective reciprocity. Communicating from the ineffective ego states invites responses from reciprocal ineffective ego states. For example, if you are critical of someone (Critical Parent), you may get a defensive response back (Rebellious Child), or the other party may seem to go along with you (Compliant Child).

You may achieve short-term results by being in Critical Parent, resulting in others being in Compliant Child. However, the state of threat created undermines their ability to think for themselves (Adult) and stores up trouble for the future as they may flip from Compliant Child to Rebellious Child or even Critical Parent. See Figure 2.6 to see how this works.

2.8 Intent and impact

Remember that your intent does not equal your impact. Just because we intend to come across from the effective ego states doesn't mean it will be perceived as such. It also depends on what ego state others are in when they hear you.

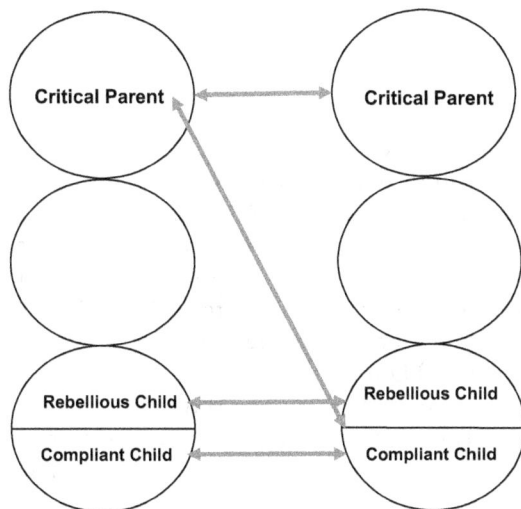

Figure 2.6 The most common ineffective reciprocal responses

If we perceive someone is communicating or behaving towards us from one of the three effective ego states, then we are more likely to respond reciprocally with one of the three effective ego states. Whereas if we perceive that someone is using one of the ineffective ego states, we are very likely to respond with a similarly ineffective ego state.

2.8.1 Perception

Perception is an important concept here: we may think we are using an effective ego state; however, if your Adult ego state is too 'tell', too full of facts, too cold, loud or monotonous, your Nurturing Parent is not curious or empathic enough, or your Free Child is over the top or inauthentic, then you may find that you have not been perceived to be in those ego states. In these situations, you are more likely to experience response from a similarly ineffective ego state, demonstrating a form of suspicion, protection or defence.

2.8.2 Increasing Ok-ness: improving effective reciprocal responses

Choosing an effective ego state, Nurturing Parent, Adult or Free Child, is important, as this choice increases the chances of being engaging, motivating and collaborating with someone else. Such a choice enhances inclusion and, as I've observed over the years, ultimately trust and followership. I genuinely believe that choosing an effective ego state is an essential choice for managing a tense or tricky conversation.

In order to communicate what we really mean and increase the chances of such clear, effective transactions, we need to engage in three key communication actions:

1. We need to consciously decrease our use of the ineffective ego states and increase our use of the effective ego states
2. We need to make our behaviours as clear as possible: in Adult we need to ask questions for clarification as much as we communicate logic and fact. We need to keep our voice tone calm showing no emotion or judgment and we need to moderate our voice tone. From Nurturing Parent, we need to be properly focused on the other person and in Free Child we need to be open and honest
3. We need to use some elements of all three effective ego states, as using only one is easily open to misinterpretation. How this happens and what to do to address this is covered in more detail in Chapter 8

2.8.3 Conflict loops: what happens when there's too many ineffective transactions

In some relationships, we may develop a pattern of behaving towards each other where the ineffective ego states are dominant. One party criticising or blaming another soon attracts an ineffective response and before too long a well-worn path becomes established. We call this a conflict loop, which, over time, becomes increasingly dysfunctional, creating a lack of OK-ness and an increased state of threat. A conflict loop can develop between individuals, between groups of people or between organisations. I address how to prevent and mange such situations in Chapter 9.

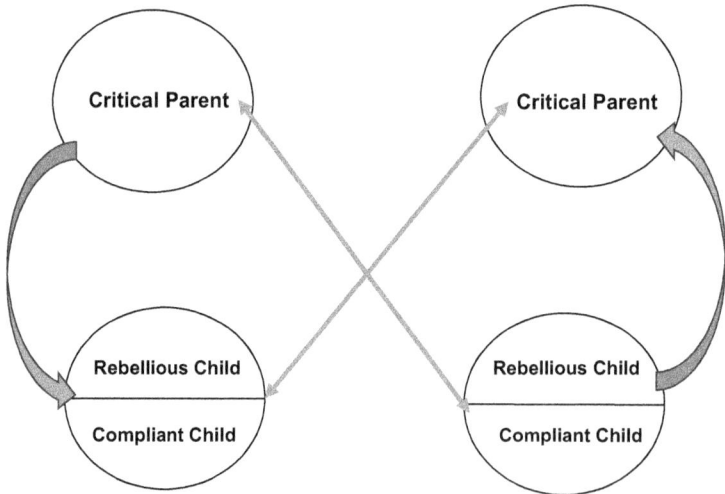

Figure 2.7 A conflict loop

2.9 Using the ego states for effective communication

To use this Organisational TA model, there are some simple steps for enhancing effective communication:

1. Recognise the ego states you communicate from most
2. Recognise the impact these are having on others
3. To engage more, increase use of the effective ego states
4. To be effective, use elements of all three effective ego states
5. Choose to decrease all the ineffective ego states
6. When you perceive an ineffective ego state in someone else, consciously choose to stay in an effective ego state to avoid conflict loops

2.10 Next steps using the ego states

This chapter has given you the basic ego state model: so far it seems very simple – for your increased effectiveness, decrease the use of ineffective ego states and increase the use of all three effective ego states. However, it's not quite as simple as that. The nuances and practical application are presented in much more detail in Section III, where I cover their use to understand relationship dynamics, how to handle disagreement and how to get the best from colleagues. Later on, in Section V, the combination section, I use the language of ego states to address giving feedback, instilling ownership and how to speak up in difficult situations.

2.11 Self-reflection

- Which ego states do you recognise you use most and least as a leader?
- Which ego states do you recognise when you are in a threat state?
- Which do you recognise when you are calm and feeling OK?
- What happens to you and colleagues in tense or tricky conversations?
- To increase your leadership effectiveness which ego state/s could you choose to do more or less of?

References

Berne, E. (1977). *Games people play: The psychology of human relationships*. Grove Press.

Harris, T. (1969). *I'm OK – you're OK: A practical guide to transactional analysis*. (1st ed.). Galahad Books.

Wagner, A. (1981). *The transactional manager: How to solve people problems with transactional analysis*. Prentice Hall.

3

MODEL 3

The psychology of how humans adapt to change: the transition tasks

I think this is the most important of the base models. For me, the context behind how humans change and adapt is the essence of understanding leadership. If you know how to engage with another person so that they are more likely to follow your thinking and engage with your new ideas or requirements, then that's leadership. Here, I build a picture of what happens to us when someone asks us to do something differently, big or small. I look at how we react and what we can do about it. I identify four psychological tasks that are needed to help to engage someone that I think are important to know. I start the chapter with a transition curve, a well-known depiction of change. I end with those psychological tasks, something you are unlikely to have come across elsewhere.

This base model demonstrates the underpinnings of every leadership action from influencing someone to do something differently to keeping them motivated and engaged. This base model is in two parts: first, I explore what happens to humans when we ask them to do something differently, in particular something they are not keen on doing; then, second, I present four psychological tasks that help ourselves and others adjust to such a change.

3.1 Part A: how humans respond to change

Many studies of workplace change show us that a key reason that organisational change is so hard is that people are resistant to change. Resistance is the uncomfortable emotional arousal created when we don't accept the new idea, expectation or organisational direction: it's a manifestation of a threat state that prevents us from attending to the reasons for the new concept and stops us seeking support from our managers or peers. Some leaders respond to these defensive behaviours with frustration, by ignoring or with annoyance and even coercion, which, in turn, results in mistrust, resentment and further resistance.

DOI: 10.4324/9781003623250-4

We call the process people go through *transition* – an internal readjustment process. It is often transition, rather than the new concept itself, that people resist. We resist:

- The discomfort that the process brings
- Giving up our sense of identity as it is currently expressed in our work
- The perceived chaos and uncertainty
- Having to learn new ways
- The risky business of new beginnings – doing what we've not done before

We go through transition every day, short-lasting ones could be an update to our software that alters where things are on the screen or a change to our priorities for the day. By the end of that day, we will have adjusted to these. Then, there are bigger, more consequential workplace transitions, such as adjusting to working with a new boss or team colleague through to facing a restructure or even potential redundancy. And, of course, let's not forget that many changes are welcome; in such situations we scoot fairly effortlessly to the other side of the process.

3.1.1 Adapting to something new

There are generally thought to be four stages to a workplace change that someone does not want:

1. Protest – characterised by denial, shock, avoidance and frustration
2. Strong emotions – demonstrated by high levels of anxiety, anger and frustration, sadness and loss and even guilt and envy. This is where resistance is most clearly seen, at worst characterised by cynicism, hostility and even sabotage
3. Reorganisation – a period of acceptance, where an individual learns new skills, has new experiences and invests in a new beginning
4. Commitment – demonstrating that we can end up happy, confident and empowered once a transition has ended

In these days of constant change, some practitioners add a fifth state, 'replay' where we emerge from one transition only to be plunged into the next.

3.1.2 The transition curve

These stages are not linear and can be re-entered at any time. They are best depicted on a transition curve. These may be familiar to you. They originate from Elizabeth Kubler-Ross's work on grief (1969); she was the first person to present this process on a curve. Since then, many exponents have lifted this concept and used it in workplace settings, thereby the transition curve has become a familiar tool describing the process of organisational change. These days all management consultants have their own: I'm no exception: the one I use is partly based on Scott and Jaffe's (1988) interpretation. They depict the process of transition on a 4 x 4 grid, making it easy to see the stages. Over the years with my colleagues at ORConsulting and, later, in my own consultancy, I've arrived at my own version. On this transition curve, morale, how one feels and confidence levels, are plotted against time.

3.1.3 Behaviours during the transition to 'newness'

At different points on the transition curve people behave in different ways. Individuals might openly express their feelings or keep them hidden. They might also be focusing on either the past or the future. The curve shows the kind of behaviour and focus expected at different points in the time of transition.

In the section at the top left of Figure 3.1, people are likely to be open about their feelings towards the change. They may *openly* state that they are not happy about what's proposed and may directly challenge it. Their behaviours are appropriate and in proportion to what they are feeling. Common reactions here are a desire to distance oneself from the perceived threat, so denial and avoidance and irritation or frustration that the change is occurring, often expressed strongly, known as dissonance. When an announcement about change is a surprise, this stage is manifested by shock responses. All of these are threat responses.

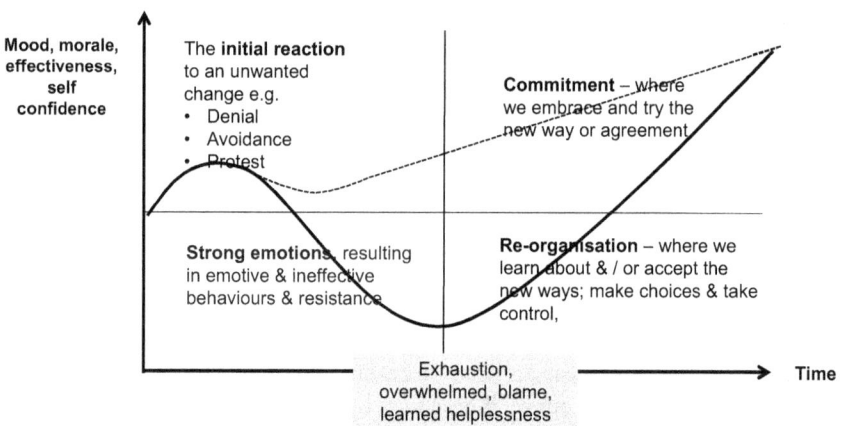

Figure 3.1 The transition curve showing how humans adjust to change

At the bottom left of Figure 3.1, people are at their most resistant. They feel negative about the new idea or change but aren't dealing with their feelings effectively. Inside they might be angry that things are changing, sad because they liked the way it was before or anxious about what's going to happen to them.

Outwardly, behaviours may be disproportionate to what they are feeling or to the scale of the change. They may have low productivity, be irritable with colleagues and blame other people for things. They may seek others who are feeling the same way and may form formidable cliques, the 'BMW Club – bitching moaning and whinging' – who are critical of those who do not see the world their way. Many feel their efforts are futile and 'just go through the motions'. At the very worst some may even engage in direct sabotage or behave in a passive aggressive way, such as with relentless cynicism. They may nostalgically hanker after the past as they feel threatened by an uncertain future.

In this phase of a transition we are often overwhelmed by sensation or emotion, we find it hard to think and be really logical or realistic. Here, our brains are in the threat state, resulting in less effective attention to other people and decreased access to the PFC, where it is hard to find a logical, solution-focused path through the situation.

Those who find it hard to progress through a transition may get stuck at the bottom. This is a very dark place where someone doesn't feel able to control or influence what is happening. This is known as 'learned helplessness' and characterised by an inability to act and a tendency to blame others for the change and the impact it is having. Sickness and burnout are common here, so preventing our colleagues getting there is paramount.

In the area at the bottom right of Figure 3.1, people are looking towards the future and have made a conscious decision to accept or adapt to the change, albeit reluctantly. They may be starting to see how the change could be positive and how it may work for them. This may be as a result of opening up to new learning or information. Outwardly, people in this area might start to ask questions about the new ways. They might experiment with working with them and experience successes and failures as they start to adapt. Rarely is this process of acceptance and new learning linear, being characterised by a 'two steps forwards and one step back' progression as we experiment, trying to take things on board and form new habits.

Neurobiologically, in this stage we are beginning to re-access our PFC, yet the process of this is intermittent at first.

In the top right part of Figure 3.1, people are becoming committed to the change. They are able to manage their behaviours and emotions effectively. They feel more positive about the change and the benefits it could bring. While the change may not have been to their liking, they have successfully navigated through it. They may even see the world more positively as a result. They feel more confident in themselves and their ability to deal with the future and whatever changes it presents. At the highest point in this quadrant

25

they are pleased that they went through the process, as the new way now seems better and has made them stronger; this is why this theoretical depiction of change ends higher than it began.

3.2 Leading change

In a well-led change, and/or a welcome change, people dealing with transition would follow the 'dotted route' on Figure 3.1. So, while they may experience strong emotions in getting to grips with the change, their emotions and behaviours are transient and 'above the line' – appropriate and proportionate to what they are experiencing. They can successfully direct their efforts to adapting to change and feel confident in their ability to deal with the future. Using the psychological tasks of transition (see below) effectively helps leaders to manage this.

Eight things to know about change and transition

1. People's perceptions and reactions to change will always be subjective and personal
2. People can experience multiple transitions at once that are likely to include personal as well as work changes concurrently
3. The path depicted by transition curves is theoretical, depicting all the possible positions. We move about on the curve very fast (or sometimes very slowly). Some of us may never experience the lows depicted here and others may not emerge in a stronger position than where they started. The curve gives us an idea of what it's like in all the possible positions
4. Therefore, we can never know for sure where people are on the transition curve (although it's a useful team activity to ask and plot)
5. Where we are on the curve ourselves will influence the way we see others and the organisation. It will influence how we behave, and lead
6. Moving through the bottom of the transition curve is not a given. It needs to be an active decision that only an individual can make. Some people can stay there for weeks and months and even years – and may not even be aware of it
7. While you need to provide the conditions for people to go along the 'dotted route', you cannot make people change if they don't want to – it's ultimately their choice and responsibility. What you can do as a leader is explain the consequences of not changing, managing and supporting them accordingly

8. In the fast-paced world we now live in we seldom have the chance to recover from a change, or even complete it before being confronted with the next one

It's important not to be frustrated or judgemental of those in the bottom left-hand side: resistance is a natural response to threat.

3.3 Part B: The psychological tasks of transition that help us to adapt to change

These have been formulated through psychologists asking thousands of people 'what helped you to come through a transition'?[1] They are the psychological actions everyone needs in order to adjust to an unwanted change.

In order to limit threat, resistance and prevent despair, people need:

- A clear sense of purpose and the direction of travel
- Supporting, acknowledgement and being understood
- Clear expectations and lines of accountability
- Trusted relationships, including someone trustworthy to lead and recognise them

I recommend the effective use of these psychological tasks, all of which build reward states and will better prepare you and your colleagues for change. Effective use of these helps us all to move through the transition curve without experiencing strong, potentially damaging, emotions.

3.3.1 The psychological tasks

The psychological tasks are presented sequentially, the idea being that we start a transition concentrating attention on the purpose. However, although we need all of the behaviours contained in all four of the psychological tasks, it is smart to focus primarily on the requirements of the quadrant we (or another) are in at that time.

If you are going through a transition, the psychological tasks help you to decide where you are and consequently what you need to do. If you have strong emotions, it is important to find someone safe to express your feelings to and appeal to for support. It is very important that leaders are aware when they are in the bottom left-hand side of Figure 3.1 as this is where poor decision making and ineffective leadership often occur. There are times when we need a clearer direction or more recognition for what we have done – if these are not forthcoming, we will need to ask for them.

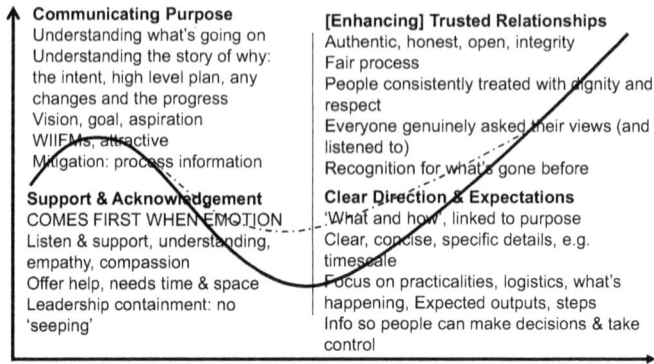

Communicating Purpose	[Enhancing] Trusted Relationships
Understanding what's going on	Authentic, honest, open, integrity
Understanding the story of why:	Fair process
the intent, high level plan, any	People consistently treated with dignity and
changes and the progress	respect
Vision, goal, aspiration	Everyone genuinely asked their views (and
WIIFMs, attractive	listened to)
Mitigation: process information	Recognition for what's gone before

Support & Acknowledgement	Clear Direction & Expectations
COMES FIRST WHEN EMOTION	'What and how', linked to purpose
Listen & support, understanding,	Clear, concise, specific details, e.g.
empathy, compassion	timescale
Offer help, needs time & space	Focus on practicalities, logistics, what's
Leadership containment: no	happening, Expected outputs, steps
'seeping'	Info so people can make decisions & take
	control

Figure 3.2 The tasks of transition that help us to adapt to change

You can use the transition curve to think about where any of your colleagues may be. The psychological tasks then help you decide what their specific requirements may be to aid them through their own transition and consequently facilitate their optimum performance.

3.3.2 The four psychological tasks of transition are described and defined as follows

3.3.2.1 Task 1: Communicating purpose

You can provide direction for people by communicating a clear purpose and vision for the way forward. It is important to describe why the change is happening, give good quality data to demonstrate your thinking and describe what the desired outcome is. To increase your effectiveness, you can communicate clearly and concisely and tailor your message to the needs of your audience. You can make sure that people have understood and are engaged with debate rather than just passively receiving information.

Specifying purpose is fundamental to human action, it is a significant prompt to developing reward states. As highly adapted beings, we need meaning to engage in something new: we need to know why. If this can be matched to someone's needs, so that it is attractive to them or presents change as a valuable opportunity, this helps. Neuroscientists have found that when there is a good purpose for something, access to the integration centre of the brain, the PFC, is enhanced, resulting in clearer thinking, better ability to problem solve and becoming actively involved in something different. Having a good purpose is one of the few ways in which PFC activity overrides limbic system stimulation

Sometimes we are unable to give all the information: for example, where it is confidential. Here, we can rely on 'process' information instead of the content: this is where we explain what the process is, explaining when and how people will gain the information rather than giving it. Even when doing this, be prepared to repeat the information many times, in different ways. In a difficult situation humans need 7–21 repetitions to properly grasp reasons for an unwanted change.

3.3.2.2 Task 2: Support and acknowledgment

Because we respond emotionally to change, often before we can properly think things through, we need to be aware of people's emotional responses. Listening and understanding to how they feel is a crucial task of managing change even when you fundamentally disagree with their response. Giving someone an emotional outlet often is the step needed to help them think about and process the change. It is now well established that when someone is experiencing a strong emotion one of the most effective actions they can do is to name the emotion. This calms the limbic system that creates the emotion allowing the PFC to dominate.

Talking with another person, actively listening to them, hearing and understanding what they are feeling, then supporting them to manage their emotions are the most important elements of how to behave within this task.

This task isn't just responding considerately to others' emotional responses, it is also about managing our own. A key activity here is becoming aware of, and acknowledging, one's own reactions, then taking steps to manage these through resilience techniques.

Having our emotional responses to change acknowledged allows the reward state to dominate and for us to be able to consider the next psychological task.

3.3.2.3 Task 3: Clear direction and expectations

Here, we begin to focus on what needs to occur; perhaps this is creating choices for ourselves, it may be making sure that someone else is very clear about what to expect or what you want them to focus on. We need to have moved out of a threat state to do this, so be sure to not neglect the previous task.

The essence of this psychological task is clarity. This means having a concise, easy to understand message about what is expected, how and when it is to be achieved. Here, you take ownership for delivery and act as a role model for your teams. As a result, you encourage someone to take accountability for their deliverables too. You ensure that people are clear what is expected of them and understand how initiatives join up so they can make decisions and assess their options for themselves.

It is perfectly possible to give a clear expectation, holding this firm while using behaviours from the previous task, being supportive, empathic and acknowledging the impact the changed expectation is having. This is an element of compassionate leadership, demonstrating the ability to be both firm and understanding at the same time.

3.3.2.4 Task 4: Enhancing trusted relationships

This task is all about ensuring there is a good quality relationship maintained during the transition, one that inspires trust and confidence. This means behaving in ways that maintain integrity, and demonstrates authenticity and warmth. Through this task, leaders involve and engage their colleagues, they remember to provide gratitude, affirmation and validation, especially for the good things that came before the change and the efforts of those going through transition and the discomfort they may be experiencing. These actions increase levels of oxytocin, the bonding neurotransmitter substance, that calms limbic system function. To deliver this task well there also needs to be perceived fairness in the message, another reward state prompt.

The essence of this task is why we follow people. We tend to follow people whom we trust, those who are authentic, who can relate to us and those who do as they say they will. They are honest with us about why they have chosen to behave and act the way they do and can explain this to us with a plausible and engaging narrative. If you think about what good leadership looks like to you, then enact these characteristics, then you are performing this task.

We depict this task at the end of the transition journey, not because it's the last task to be completed but to demonstrate it's the one that pulls us the furthest. With a good relationship in place, we're far more likely to quickly progress along the dotted line. So in some respects this is the one we need to have in place first.

3.3.3 Past and future

When we are in the left-hand side quadrants of Figure 3.1 we are still focused on the past, the way it was, the previous boss, system or administration. Using all the psychological tasks helps people to move to the future focused space, the right-hand side quadrants, where they can consider what the change really means, realistically consider whether they want to be part of it and how they will adapt. The sooner we can help people to move from past (left) to future (right) the better, as this avoids the despair and learned helplessness of the lowest point of the curve.

3.3.4 The order matters

A golden rule when using the tasks is to start with the two relationally based tasks when someone is in the bottom left-hand side (Figure 3.1) of transition. When we pile on information to people who can't think straight, whose

PFCs are not accessible, then we are not heard and the information we are imparting is distorted and resistance and suspicion is more likely.

3.4 Self-reflection

- Where are you on the transition curve at the moment?
- Have you ever been in the bottom left-hand side (Figure 3.1)? What was it like? What helped you to get yourself out? Does the answer to this last question have characteristics of the four tasks?
- Where are members of your team, your peers and even your boss? Are any in the bottom left hand-side (Figure 3.1)?
- What can you do, what actions or tasks can you provide, to help any colleague move to the right hand-side of the curve?

You will recognise the four psychological tasks of transition as we progress as they are essential in many effective leadership actions. In particular, you'll see them again when we consider how to steer people through a change process in Chapter 9 and how to influence in Chapter 10.

Note

1 The psychological tasks come from the psychological consultancies Organisation Resource and ORConsulting. Psychologists devised the four tasks after hundreds of repetitions of the question 'What did you need when you went through transition?' These were originally known as the 'four building blocks of transition'. They were first published in Pearlman-Shaw (2016)

References

Kübler-Ross, E. (1969). *On death and dying: what the dying have to teach doctors, nurses, clergy and their own families.* Macmillan.
Pearlman-Shaw, K. (2016). More than a feeling. *Coaching at Work, 11*(1), 50–51. TOOLBOX: TRIED & TESTED – EMOTIONS BASED CHANGE FACILITATION – Coaching at Work https://www.coaching-at-work.com/2016/01/05/toolbox-tried-tested-emotions-based-change-facilitation/
Scott, C.D., & Jaffe, D.T. (1988, April). Survive and thrive in times of change. *Training & Development Journal, 42*(4), 25–28. https://link.gale.com/apps/doc/A6682063/AONE?u=anon~af122a88&sid=googleScholar&xid=e1ce4f75

Section II

APPLYING THE NEUROBIOLOGY

To get the best from this section you will need to read Chapter 1, 'The Neurobiology of Leadership', which covers the application of up-to-date neurobiology to leadership behaviour. Here, I use those concepts to consider how to stay resilient and avoid burnout, how to get the best from someone else and keep their brain working well at work, how to avoid the tired brain – so how to manage in limited time, and finally how to work with diversity – the neurobiology of inclusion.

DOI: 10.4324/9781003623250-5

4

HOW DO I KEEP MY BRAIN WORKING AT WORK? THE NEUROBIOLOGY OF RESILIENCE

Avoiding burnout in today's workplace

This chapter is all about how to keep the brain in a reward state: so how to ensure your brain is working well at work. I look at minimising threats, what we can do to prevent the limbic system from becoming overwhelmed and how to access the prefrontal cortex even under pressure. I consider the role of different types of social support and the vital need for purpose. I introduce a four-factor model based on up-to-date neuroscience; having all of these factors in place will support effective leadership and contribute to colleagues' well-being.

In Chapter 1, my concluding comment was that 'everything in this book is based on the principle of threat and reward: every method that follows is to help you to get yourself out of threat and into reward and do the same for those you lead and interact with'. This chapter covers four key reward building (and threat decreasing) methods that have been found to be crucial for our resilience.

A dictionary definition of resilience is 'the ability to cope with pressure and bounce back from challenges and setbacks'. When our resilience slips, we experience this as stress, which is a state of emotional strain or tension resulting from adverse or demanding circumstances. In other words, we are in a state of 'threat'. Time spent stressed affects our well-being and performance. Prolonged stress, in the worst case scenario, can lead to burnout, defined by the World Health Organization (2019) as an 'occupational phenomenon' characterised by physical and emotional exhaustion.

In order to address and build leadership resilience, I use a model that I've designed that clusters neuroscience findings about how to keep the brain working well. It was originally inspired by the work of David Rock and Dan Siegel and structured similarly to Carey Cooper's resilience model (Cooper et al., 2013; Rock et al., 2012). I've kept updating the neuroscience as this has emerged. My model has four key areas that help us to maintain and build our resilience. People who are highly resilient have strengths in all four key areas:

DOI: 10.4324/9781003623250-6

1. Have a purpose for everything that they do
2. Strategies to keep the limbic system from becoming overloaded
3. Social support
4. Strategies to keep the PFC accessible when experiencing threat

4.1 Have a purpose for everything

Having a purpose for whatever we do, especially one that is aligned to our values, to what we do and want to achieve in life, helps a great deal when we are addressing a task or a change. Simon Sinek, whose TED talk on the subject (2009) is said to be one of the most watched of all time, tells us that focusing on 'why' rather than 'what or how' creates more engagement. He advocates this as a key sales and brand technique. Furthermore, thinking about and having a good purpose for something is thought to switch on the PFC and aligned pathways far more than what or how thinking. There are far more neurons that have been shown to override emotional responses going from the PFC to the limbic system that are activated in this way.

Therefore, having a purpose for everything we do creates less threat and more reward: less limbic system stimulation, less emotion, less internal conflict and helps us to be focused and address stressors, staying resilient. There are different levels of purpose we can address, such as:

1. Higher, the overarching organisational purpose
2. Collective, why *we* are doing this
3. Personal, an attractive reason for an individual to engage in the task. This may be to pursue a wanted opportunity, or to avoid something bad happening. For people with very strong values it helps if the purpose is values aligned

Similarly, we have a number of different purposes in coming to work; it helps to be able to anchor our responses in a good purpose. These may be:

• Simply to pay the mortgage and the bills
• To do something meaningful
• To help others or to play a part in creating a better product or society
• To play a part in an organisational strategy or vision that we believe in

A recent study from McKinsey in 2021 showed that only 65% could articulate their purpose at work (Dhingra et al., 2021). I challenge the leaders I work with to link their everyday actions to a good purpose – this applies to everything from writing reports to holding meetings. How often have you been sitting in a meeting, or a section of that meeting, that has little obvious purpose for you? This is a demotivating, energy sapping experience. A leader can help others into the reward state by being aware of this and creating more purpose for them.

I was asked by a leadership group recently what leadership theme I talk about most: it's this. The eagle-eyed of you will have noticed that the communication of purpose is an essential action in each of my three base models:

- In neurobiology having a good purpose inoculates us against threats, enabling the limbic system to be less stimulated
- In the ego state model, communicating your own purpose is a key Free Child form of communication that increases the likelihood of a Free Child or Nurturing Parent response, so increases the likelihood that both you and the other person can stay in the reward state, enhancing engagement
- Purpose is one of the four transition tasks. It's the starting point in asking for any change. It is unlikely any human will embark on anything different if they don't have a clear and relevant purpose

4.2 Self-reflection

- Do you have meaningful purpose for your work?
- Can you tune into the purpose of every task you do?
- Can you increase the sense of purpose for those who work for you?

4.3 Strategies to keep the limbic system from becoming overloaded

This is a set of strategies for calming the limbic system, creating a reward state. This means being able to address negative emotions and is underpinned by our physical well-being and self-care:

4.3.1 Managing negative emotions

Evidence from neuroscience demonstrates that there are some simple, in the moment strategies we can use to increase our emotional resilience, although we still do need to sort out the underlying issue at a later time. Try these simple strategies:

1. Emotional naming: describing an emotion out loud. Naming the emotion you are experiencing out loud has been shown to dampen any further emotional stimulation in the hypothalamus. This only works if it's a concise description: telling the whole dramatic story or embellishing only stimulates and heightens the emotional response

2. Listening to others then being empathic also decreases limbic system activity and creates oxytocin due the connection we make with another

3. Mindfulness, or mental rest, has a very strong impact on decreasing stimulation in our limbic system. Mindfulness is very popular just now. Essentially, and in this context, this is when we switch off from the all the noise around us and focus on what is actually going on. This is about properly watching what's going on internally and around us without judging or reacting. At work it has been demonstrated that just a few minutes of mindfulness can:
   • Calm us down
   • Enable us to think more clearly, engaging our PFC and making more effective decisions and choices
   • Help us to feel more in control
   • Manage time more effectively
   It's particularly important for our resilience, as this activity has been found to increase oxytocin by stimulating a specific somatosensory area of the brain. This is a very important form of emotional self-management

4. If you find mindfulness hard, there are other forms of mental rest that have a similar impact. One of these is being outside or being close to nature. This decreases amygdala activity and has a big effect on the creation of positive moods that counterbalance limbic system stimulation. Other forms of mental rest that have been found to have a similar but less strong impact are reading, listening to music or watching TV for pleasure and exercise (Hammond, 2020)

These aren't the only emotional management techniques; you will already have several of your own. Using these before the emotion gets to and passes your personal threshold, the point at which you are unable to hold it back, is also important to maintain and increase your resilience.

Once you've passed your personal emotional threshold, the limbic system is in overload and you are firmly in the threat state. There are still plenty of techniques to use to 'come down': here is a small selection, each designed to ultimately 'soothe' the limbic system:

• Know how long it takes you to come down: for some it's a few minutes or hours, for others it's a few days, depending on the event that's caused the stimulation. Only take holding action in the time until you can engage your PFC. For example, if it takes you a day to start to assess what went on and what to do, don't reply to e-mails on the subject or engage the other person on that topic in that 24-hour period

• Saying your emotions out loud and being heard becomes even more important when we are highly stressed: this may be to a confidante, mentor or coach. If you don't like speaking with others try journalling;

in this case, writing about what has upset you works very well to decrease limbic system overload

- Write the angry e-mail to get the thoughts and emotions out BUT don't send it: put it in your drafts folder and review it later. It's likely to be in Critical Parent or Rebellious Child: you can amend or delete it later
- Try embodiment techniques: focus on where you sense the emotion in your body and focus on relaxing that area
- Try the techniques in the 'adaptability' section below: these are techniques to restore accessibility to our PFC

4.3.2 Self-care and well-being

Two types of self-care are vital to resilience, exercise and sleep. *Exercise* impacts the brain's blood flow, its 'plasticity', the connectivity of different brain regions and the creation of neurotransmitters. These processes depend on movement. Any kind of aerobic exercise has been shown to increase intellectual performance. Replicated studies show that exercise before work or in a lunch break increases concentration, ability to take on a bigger workload and boosts motivation. With high impact aerobic activity there's the added benefit of releasing endorphins – the brain's pain killers and mood boosters.

Sleep: How well we sleep is thought to be the biggest correlate of resilience. Lack of sleep particularly effects how much time we can spend in the slow, deliberate brain: we make more assumptions and are more biased when we don't sleep well. A tired brain has less blood flow in the PFC. And we consolidate material memories to our long-term memory storage areas during different phases of our sleep cycle.

A controversial book by Matthew Walker (2018) provides a damning critique on our lack of sleep in the western world. Walker provides evidence that 'sleep is the universal health care provider', listing a range of health benefits of sleep, from keeping slim to protecting us from nasty diseases and safeguarding our mental health.

Top of his list of what we can do is decrease caffeine: he attacks caffeine for interfering with our sleep as it decreases the neurotransmitter adenosine which creates 'sleep pressure': it promotes sleep and suppresses arousal. 'The masking agent caffeine is the most used and abused psychoactive stimulant in the world'. He advises no caffeine seven hours before we go to bed, as the half-life of caffeine is 50%, it will still be in our system at bedtime.

He damns the rise in LED light: he argues we need dark to sleep as dark stimulates the pineal gland to produce melatonin. Paying attention to digital devices, sleeping with an LED alarm clock and reading from a Kindle before bed all change this process. He cites a study of reading by iPad regularly before bed that revealed it only took a week for the melatonin production to be put back by 90 mins.

And he damns alcohol as a sleep suppressor: it fragments sleep and it supresses REM sleep, the dream sleep, a vital consolidation activity. So, he advises no alcohol after lunch.

If you are interested, he has 12 guidelines to follow to increase our sleep and consequently our resilience.

Sleep is a highly researched area with, what seems to me to be, constantly changing outcomes. I'm always hearing a new fact about sleep on various media. What's important here is to create the conditions for getting the best possible night's sleep that's right for you.

4.4 Self-reflection

- What are your emotional and management techniques?
- What are the quick ones that you can do easily at work?
- What works for you best after a 'bad' day?
- Where could you build in mental rest or mini breaks?
- Could you change your sleep or exercise routines?

4.5 Social support

The strongest correlate of workplace resilience is the amount and quality of social support. Over and over psychologists are finding that people who have good workplace confidantes, a good support system and someone to BMW ('bitch, moan and whinge') with are the most resilient. This is especially true for extroverts, who externally process their thinking and so need others to do this with. Introverts need social support too; this is more about the quality of support than the amount, as introverts internally process their thinking, needing space and time before expressing their thoughts.

There are two relevant neural pathways operating here: the first is the power of the neurotransmitter substance oxytocin, the 'attachment or bonding' chemical. When we have good interactions with others we secrete oxytocin that subdues the limbic system. It's difficult to define a good quality interaction as this will be personal to you. Often it's someone who listens, understands and empathises; for others' it's someone to jointly solve a technical problem with.

The second pathway is created by joyful or funny times with others. 'Serious play' and connecting have been found to be very important at work as this is dopamine enhancing. Essentially, this is about the importance of having fun at work. Key reward centres are stimulated when we are having fun and joking around. All kinds of things have been shown to stimulate this response from admiring aesthetics to having a good experience, from being with people we like to engaging in activities where we are rewarded and valued. Basically, anything that creates happiness and joy.

If we have the right kind of social support then these mechanisms are intact, enhancing and maintaining our resilience. When they are not, when there are too few confidantes, too many 'social drainers' or 'heart-sink' direct reports, our social support balance is damaged, and we are less resilient as a result. It is important to balance your social support so that social drainage doesn't dominate.

4.6 Self-reflection

- Is your social support balanced?
- Do you have the right types of social support?
- Where social drainage is greater than social support where can you adjust the balance?

4.7 Strategies to keep the PFC accessible when experiencing threat

Contemporary leadership models strongly demonstrate that people who can both flex their leadership style and their thinking make the best leaders. Being able to be mentally flexible, having the ability to think balanced and non-biased thoughts, thereby maintaining a positive can-do mindset, is another key correlate of good resilience. In other words, having your PFC accessible so that you can turn on the analytic or empathic networks when required. Essentially this is all about having some control over our busy brains and creating time to properly think and thereby react appropriately. There are many ways to do this, I cover four of my favourites below. Before that a word about how we think.

We have two key types of thinking:

1. Higher level thinking, also called 'thinking slow' or deliberate thinking: this is slow, concentrated, deep thought where we think carefully and in depth about what to do or analyse how or why something is
2. Fast, automatic, biased thinking, called 'thinking fast'. The fast parts of our brain like patterns: routines where they can do things quickly not calling on the slow, energy intensive system. Few of these fast processes are conscious as the fast system filters out a great deal and doesn't check the evidence, it cuts corners, it makes mistakes

This is the ground-breaking work of Daniel Kahneman from his book *Thinking Fast and Slow* (2012).

To stay resilient, to maintain a balanced mindset where the PFC is in control, we need to have a good balance of fast and slow, certainly not be dominated by fast thoughts.

4.7.1 Keeping the PFC in charge – maintaining access to slow thinking

It takes a while to get to slow thinking, we need time and uninterrupted space to get there. Once there we can stay for 20–40 minutes. This means that we need to be organised about our time management. We know that people who organise their time so that they have dedicated thinking space are more productive than those who don't. Being well organised, knowing your priorities for the day are key. There are now countless studies showing how easily disrupted we are when we multitask: for example, a paper published by Skowronek et al. in 2023 suggested that merely knowing that our phone is nearby reduces cognitive performance, working speed and overall attention.

Another way to approach this is to be solutions focused: when it's stressful concentrating on solutions instead of concerns or worries can enhance PFC access, so keeping us thinking rationally. We know that limbic system activity decreases when we are clear about what we are doing and have a plan. Furthermore, psychologists have known for years that any form of anxiety is better dealt with a plan (and a plan B): this is the basis for anxiety management techniques.

Managing access to the PFC is really all about having time to stop and think.

4.7.2 Managing negative thinking – managing fast, automatic thinking

We need to train our brains to check for automatic thoughts. This begins with reminding ourselves that we may be biased, may have made a rapid judgement or assumption too quickly, we may have made what Aeron T. Beck, the 'father' of Cognitive Behaviour Therapy (CBT) called a 'thought error' (Beck et al., 1979). Such illogical thinking causes us more limbic system stimulation, increases the strength of negative emotions and changes our communication where we are far more likely to be communicating in the ineffective than the effective ego states. Evidential based thinking is a well-known technique from CBT that trains us to check for the evidence: for example, why someone communicated as they did, whether someone is treating us unfairly or whether we've really been forgotten about. Train your brain to ask yourself evidence based questions then act on your responses.

Useful evidence checking questions to ask yourself are:

What is the evidence?

- What evidence do I have to support my thoughts?
- What evidence do I have against them?

What are the biases in my thinking about myself?

- Am I condemning myself on the basis of a single event?
- Am I attending to all the available data?
- Am I concentrating too much on my weaknesses and not on my strengths?
- Am I paying too much attention to the people who think like me, not those who don't?
- Am I only seeing the negatives in this situation and not the positives, even if these are small?
- Am I expecting something bad to happen or overestimating the chances of disaster?
- Am I expecting too much of myself here?

What is the effect of thinking the way that I do?

- Does it help me or hinder me?
- What would be the impact of looking at things more positively or with less bias?

What alternative views are there?

- How would a compassionate colleague view this situation?
- Am I assuming that this perspective is the only one possible?

What action can I take?

- How can I put a more balanced perspective in place?
- Am I overlooking solutions to problems based on an assumption that they won't work?

4.7.3 The breakout principle

How many times have you pushed yourself to finish that e-mail or complete that report by working right up to the deadline and run into your next activity? This can be avoided. Neuroscientists have discovered the importance of switching the brain off for a bit when doing hard work. This can be anything from daydreaming to doing another task for a while. While we're having this time out, we're letting the brain catch up: in these moments specific pathways switch on, thereby integrating neural activity from disparate parts of the brain allowing the PFC to do that integration for us unconsciously. In other words, the brain can keep that thinking going in the background, on automatic, while we get on with something else.

Another tip for allowing yourself to be adaptable is about using your brain's energy wisely. This will also save you time. Leaving that thinking task halfway through, knowing you're going to come back to it in the next 24 hours allows you to be more adaptable to your current environment. And the quality of that thinking is likely to be just as good or even better as the brain has had more time to process it.

4.7.4 The 'energy paradigm'

Jim Loehr and Tony Schwartz published a seminal book, *The Power of Full Engagement* (2003). This challenged how we work and live, introducing the idea of the 'essence' of high performance which, at its heart, is how we manage our energy.

How much are you fully engaged with whatever mission you are on? Are you eager to get to work, happy and ready to walk through the door at home and fulfilled enough to get a good night's sleep? Loehr and Schwartz suggest that we consider our energy use during the day as a precious resource. It's not about time management but about managing energy, where the ability to expend, then recover, energy is crucial in meeting one's goals. They suggest that we need to learn to balance energy expenditure with intermittent energy renewal. To do so, we have to find positive energy rituals – highly specific routines for managing energy. These rituals may need some willpower, we may have to force ourselves, for example, to be mindful, have that tea break or go for a walk in order to replenish energy.

Consider what drains your energy, then think about what you need to do to recover or renew your energy so that you can function as much as possible with the high positive energy you need. In particular, if you have just been in a high energy using meeting or other situation, then what energy replenishing ritual do you need before you can go into the next one?

4.8 Self-reflection

* Do you have dedicated time to think?
* What would help you to concentrate better?
* Could you be even more organised?
* How could you control your inner chatter? Which evidence-based questions could you use more often?
* Which adaptability strategy to keep your PFC working better and your brain in the reward state is best for you?
* When could you experiment with the breakout principle?
* How and when could you replenish your energy more?

4.9 Resilience action planning

We need all four resilience building elements to build or stay resilient, maintaining reward states. Now consider whether you have something

Table 4.1 Resilience action planning matrix

HAVE PURPOSE	PREVENT LIMBIC SYSTEM OVERLOAD
Do you have meaningful purpose for your work? Can you tune into the purpose of every task you do? Can you increase the sense of purpose for those who work for you	What are your emotional and management techniques? What are the quick ones that you can do easily at work? What works for you best after a 'bad' day? Where could you build in mental rest or mini breaks? Could you change your sleep or exercise routines?
SOCIAL SUPPORT	KEEP PFC ACCESSIBLE
Is your social support balanced? Do you have the right types of social support? Where social drainage is greater than social support where can you adjust the balance?	Do you have dedicated time to think? What would help you to concentrate better? Could you be even more organised? How could you control your inner chatter? Which evidence-based questions could you use more often? When could you experiment with the breakout principle? How and when could you replenish your energy more?

covered from all four elements. Use this matrix to consider what you can do differently, to stop, start and continue to enhance your resilience.

If you want a more detailed approach of the neurobiology and how to use it, I recommend Caroline Webb's great book, *How To Have A Good Day* (2016).

References

Beck, A.T., Rush, A.J., Shaw, B.F., & Emery, G. (1979). *Cognitive therapy of depression.* Guilford Press.

Cooper, C.L., Flint-Taylor, J., & Pearn, M. (2013). What individuals can do: Strengthening the four personal resilience resources. In: *Building resilience for success*, pp. 115–144. Palgrave Macmillan. https://doi.org/10.1057/9781137367839_6

Dhingra, N., Samo, A., Schaninger, B., & Schrimper, M. (2021). *Help your employees find purpose – or watch them leave.* McKinsey & Company. https://www.mckinsey.com/~/media/mckinsey/business%20functions/people%20and%20organizatio nal%20performance/our%20insights/help%20your%20employees%20find%20 purpose%20or%20watch%20them%20leave/help-your-employees-find-purp ose-or-watch-them-leave.pdf

Hammond, C. (2020). *The art of rest: How to find respite in the modern age.* Canongate Books.

Kahneman, D. (2012). *Thinking, fast and slow.* Penguin.

Loehr, J., & Schwartz, T. (2003). *The power of full engagement: managing energy not time is the key to high performance and personal renewal.* Simon and Schuster.

Rock, D., Siegel, D.J., Poelmans, S., Payne, J. (2012, October). The healthy mind platter. *Neuroleadership Journal*, *4*, 1–23. https://www.omgaanmetparkinson.nl/wp-content/uploads/2014/10/The-Healthy-Mind-Platter.pdf

Sinek, S. (2009, 29 September). *How great leaders inspire action*. [Video]. YouTube. https://www.ted.com/talks/simon_sinek_how_great_leaders_inspire_action?utm_campaign=tedspread&utm_medium=referral&utm_source=tedcomshare

Skowronek, J., Seifert, A., & Lindberg, S. (2023). The mere presence of a smartphone reduces basal attentional performance. *Scientific Reports*, *13*, 9363. https://doi.org/10.1038/s41598-023-36256-4

Walker, M. (2018). *Why we sleep: The new science of sleep and dreams*. Penguin.

Webb, C. (2016). *How to have a good day: The essential toolkit for a productive day at work and beyond*. Pan Macmillan.

World Health Organization (2019, 28 May). *Burn-out an "occupational phenomenon*. *International Classification of Diseases*. https://www.who.int/news/item/28-05-2019-burn-out-an-occupational-phenomenon-international-classification-of-diseases

5

HOW DO I GET THE BEST FROM SOMEONE? UNDERSTANDING INDIVIDUAL NEUROBIOLOGY

Avoiding threat and building rewards:
the seven types

Everyone responds to a different profile of threats and rewards. We all have different prompts for threat and respond to different actions that create reward. Understanding different people's threats and rewards is very helpful so that leaders can choose whether to meet these to get the best from their colleagues. In this chapter I outline the seven threat prompts and reward types that I think have most relevance in the workplace and then explore how to use these to get the best from coworkers and to create the environment to get these for yourself too.

We all respond to different threat prompts; this is due to a mixture of our personality types, our experiences and our learning, and differs in different situations. Knowing what we react to and what others react to, as well as what calms us, is important information, not only useful in leading, but also for all our relationships. Creating reward states for ourselves and others is how we get the best out of each other. In reward states, also known as 'positive strokes' (see Chapter 10), we secrete key neurotransmitter substances that keep our PFC working: these are oxytocin, dopamine, serotonin and the endorphins.

5.1 Threat prompts

In the workplace we will avoid situations where our specific threat prompts are more likely, becoming emotional, defensive, more biased and/or ineffective in our behaviours.[1] Common examples are being overloaded, having a difficult conversation with a colleague, receiving a stinging email or unfair feedback. Neuroscientists describe these moments as experiencing 'social pain', similar to how we experience physical pain and in all cases such stimulation fires the limbic areas which, in turn, causes us to secrete adrenaline and cortisol. Through this model the idea is to recognise your own and others'

DOI: 10.4324/9781003623250-7

threat prompts, then do the opposite, provide rewards, as these change the brain state, meaning that we and others can function optimally and more effectively.

All threat prompts have matching actions that prevent or minimise the threat, more likely to create reward. Once we know these it will be possible to recognise at least two threat prompts and a wide range of needed reward actions.

5.2 Reward types

These are the opposite of the threat prompts. For each threat there are actions that build reward, lower limbic system stimulation and overload, thereby creating access to the two key networks we need to lead that are located in the PFC:

1. The analytic system (or default mode network), where we can integrate various data from around the brain and deal with complexity
2. The empathic network (or task positive network), which allows us to process emotions, connect, attach to others as well as having a role in our ability to be empathic

By providing more of these reward behaviours, or positive strokes, for ourselves and others, we are able to function and perform better at work (and in general in life).

There are many different actions that trigger threat or create rewards. A number or authors have categorised these, such as David Rock in his SCARF model (2008) and Sue France (2022). I have identified seven threat prompts and reward types, described below, that I think have the most relevance at work.

Threat prompts and reward types

1. Validation, recognition and affirmation
2. Control, agency and predictability
3. Support, acknowledgement and being heard
4. Having a good purpose
5. Belonging
6. Success, achievement and outcome focused
7. Equality

As you are reading these, think about:

- Which are your threat prompts, what precipitates threat for you?
- What creates reward for you, enabling you to lead and function effectively?
- What do you recognise in the people around you?

5.3 The seven threat prompts and reward types

5.3.1 Validation, recognition and affirmation

When we are validated for our efforts, recognised or thanked for our contributions or affirmed for our skills, we can secrete all of those key neurotransmitter substances. These play a large part in keeping our limbic areas calm and the PFC accessible. How we perform and how this is noticed or valued is likely to be important.

Threats are many and could include a lack of validation or gratitude in situations where these are hoped for or expected, a sense of no longer having relevance or not being seen for our contribution, experience or skills. These situations cause anger, hurt and resentment. Long-term absence of recognition causes conflict and passive-aggressive responses in the recipient.

Rewards are specifically about providing recognition, gratitude and validation. This may be through positive feedback, public acknowledgment or some form of actual reward. It is also important that when working with someone with a validation threat not to override them publicly, creating a positive frame for why things are happening. Some people need more recognition and validation than others, some people need very little: it's important to work out who needs what sort of validation, and how much, to get the best from them. This is the art of providing the right amount and type of positive strokes (see Chapter 10). Replicated studies show that increasing gratitude can increase happiness by up to 400% (Seligman, 2011).

5.3.2 Control, agency and predictability

The brain is a great prediction machine and likes order, for some people more than others.

Threat: feeling out of control, having little perceived agency is a key threat for many, causing them to spiral, become anxious and angry. Common workplace precipitators are change, overload, uncertainty about the future or too many competing demands. Here, our limbic system fires, making us avoid the change or attack the person who brings the change. Just a small amount of uncertainty precipitates a pattern recognition mechanism in our occipital cortex telling us something doesn't fit – we prefer to be able to predict the pattern.

Micromanagement is another common control threat prompt, where one's control literally feels threatened. Also important here are the workplace systems and structures around us, when these don't work well they create stress.

Reward: creating reward to counterbalance this category of threats includes ensuring someone has control over something so they have choices about how they do their work; it's about letting people make decisions for themselves. Or it may be filling in gaps to provide clarity. This is why the information you give is so important, as it can create predictability and a sense of certainty. Helping people to be on top of their work, helping them with organisational processes and systems, can be a key control enhancer too.

5.3.3 Support, acknowledgement and being heard

These are key leadership actions in times of change, much needed for successful engagement and influence. When we feel we are being heard and understood, it increases the connectivity in neural fibres that are crucial for bringing together disparate brain areas for increased cognitive function.

Threat: one of the commonest complaints about a difficult boss is their lack of empathy, compassion or understanding, key threats for many. The frustration that mounts when we don't feel heard is a key cause of social pain. Common threats here would be being judged, criticised, excluded, put down or ignored, all sadly common in the workplace. These may not be meant but they are perceived with impact. Responses to such leadership behaviours are likely to be defensive or a lack of true engagement, a false compliance, so Rebellious or Compliant Child. These actions are commonly the underlying cause of grievances, a spiralling loss of trust or engagement.

Reward: underlying this threat/reward mechanism is the role of oxytocin: when we form a good relationship with another human we secrete this substance, which keeps the limbic system calm, creating the state of reward. Key facets of good human relationships are the ability to listen actively, hear and understand what someone's experience is and offer some form of empathy, compassion or support, all oxytocin building actions. Some people need this more than others, some of us manage with very little. If you are not good at providing these empathic actions they can be learnt.

If you think that listening and properly understanding means that you won't be able to hold firm, think again, it is quite possible to listen properly to someone and have an effective, engaging dialogue about why something needs doing a specific way: this happens when the other person is really heard first. In such situations you never know, there may be an even better solution to your problem or idea, through properly hearing you find a better way.

5.3.4 Having a good purpose

As discussed in Chapter 4, purpose has a unique neurobiological function: when we are connected with a good purpose the PFC works well, even when there is high limbic system activity. Purpose seems to act as a calming factor.

Threat: without a good purpose for something, threat mechanisms lead us to disengage and disagree. Humans will engage in something new for a good purpose – if it's attractive, even better. Without this we feel disorientated, confused, unsure and even coerced. We will avoid engaging, are more likely to procrastinate and, in the absence of information, human beings make up their own reasons for something, usually negatively. The absence of purpose can lead to suspicion.

Reward: ensuring you give someone a good purpose for what you are asking is key. As mentioned in Chapter 4, there are different levels of purpose, any of which can create this crucial connection, such as:

- Higher: the overarching organisational purpose
- Collective: why *we* are doing this
- Personal: an attractive reason for an individual to engage in the ask

It is, therefore, important to take the time to find a purpose that you believe in for what you are being asked to do, and, when leading, provide a good purpose for others; even describing your own purpose can help here, too.

5.3.5 Belonging

This is another oxytocin enhancer, ultimately calming the limbic system. Exclusion, the opposite, increases our stress hormones, cortisol, adrenaline and, in men, testosterone, all causing threat responses with higher emotional arousal, unhappiness and often an increase in conflict.

Threat: a lack of belonging can be experienced as being in the 'out 'group; this may be not being included in the joke, meetings or social events that a person is unable to attend or where there are cliques in a team. This threat is triggered when we feel rejected or isolated, consequently leading to feelings of loneliness at work, where we feel disconnected from others.

We know the impact of exclusion in organisations: attrition increases, productivity falls, grievances are more common, collective team perform-ance falls as does team cohesion.

Reward: increasing belonging requires making an extra effort to include. Studies of inclusive leaders by Bourke and Titus (2020) show us that there are six key leadership behaviours needed to properly include.

Bourke and Titus's six inclusive leadership behaviours

1. Making a visible commitment to inclusion
2. Curiosity
3. Awareness of bias
4. Being humble about one's failings
5. Observant and respective of other cultures
6. Creating a collaborative approach

We need to engage in activities where we fit in. The more oxytocin we have, the better we perform, so creating social interaction for those who need it or ensuring people don't have to work alone are key reward mechanisms here. Even if we can't create predictability and control, or even purpose, by engaging in these leadership activities we can increase inclusivity and belonging in teams.

5.3.6 Success, achievement and outcome focused

Some of us are more motivated by outcomes. This mechanism is all about dopamine responses: when we succeed or achieve, we secrete dopamine, a neurotransmitter substance that masks social pain.

Threat: In the brain the pain and pleasure systems work together, creating a balance mechanism. A dopamine hit from an achievement leads to pleasure but then the brain levels this. Each hit of pleasure is followed by some pain which we experience as cravings. In the workplace we can experience this as the need to achieve more, to move on, to the solve the next problem, to focus on the outcome. We can become consumed by the need to achieve. Modern-day workplaces reinforce this. As leaders we can be seduced by the need to focus on, and drive, outcomes where we don't properly assess what is the most important priority. This creates very pressured, overloaded environments for ourselves and colleagues where we multi-task, trying to do too much at once. All of this means that our limbic system is overloaded and we can't access the analytic network in our PFCs to order and coordinate tasks.

Rewards here are about achieving the balance without the cravings; this way, the PFC can assess the task, decide which successes are best to aim for and come up with a plan to do this. The essential element of creating a reward state for this type is to create thinking time to construct plans and an order for meaningful successes. Help yourself and others to focus on key achievements, help them to chunk their plans into steps and stages and avoid multi-tasking. Give people time and space to properly focus.

Multiple studies demonstrate that the most effective people are those who are well organised. This is because they are able to access and use their analytic network in their PFC. Having a plan with rewards embedded at each chunk helps to be more solution and outcome focused (for more on how to do this see Chapter 6).

5.3.7 Equality

Equality and fairness matter a great deal in the workplace. In surveying hundreds of groups across my programmes, I've observed that this is the number one cause of threat states in the workplaces I visit.

Threat: when someone perceives or decides that something is unjust or unbalanced, the response can be strong. This is a key reason why your co-workers may not be engaging. Not being seen as fair, perhaps not having fulfilled what others expected you to do, can lead to conflicted, angry and positional behaviours from your direct reports. Or perhaps it's what causes you to take a stance.

Reward: Ensuring that you're using, and demonstrating, a just process and are being impartial prevents anger, resentment and disengagement. Fairness is created through clear, authentic reciprocal communications, ensuring processes are explicit and kept to. This means creating time to explain what's happening and being prepared to repeat your reasoning. Many years ago, when in clinical practice, I learnt that it takes someone in an established threat state 7–21 repetitions to hear a difficult message.

In addition there are four factors of fairness to check for:

- Is the process fair?
- Are the outcomes fair?
- Are explanations shared?
- Are the people treated fairly, with dignity and respect?

5.5 Using threat prompts and reward types

You will notice some crossover between these threat prompts and reward types: for example, exclusion is a factor in both belonging and support and acknowledgment, organisation is important in both control and being outcomes focused. When deciding where you and others sit, focus on the underlying need. In this case, is exclusion more about needing to belong to a group or more simply being heard by another; is better organisation going to help create clarity and certainty or aid good quality outcome achievement?

Because threat prompts are so detrimental, we need to build reward mechanisms into our leadership practice for our own increased effectiveness and the optimal performance of our teams. Eminent psychologists working in this field, Richard Boyzatis et al. (2019), says that we need to increase rewards over threat by a ratio of 3:1 or even 5:1.

5.6 Self-reflection

- Which are your threat prompts, what precipitates threat for you?
- What creates reward for you, enabling you to lead effectively?
- What do you recognise are threat prompts and reward types for the people around you?
- Think of the most difficult person you lead, what could be their threat prompts and reward types? Could you experiment with creating less threat and more reward for them?

Note

1 'Threat prompts' and 'reward types' are terms used exclusively by Kate Pearlman-Shaw.

References

Bourke, J., & Titus, A. (2020, March 6). The key to inclusive leadership. *Harvard Business Review*. https://hbr.org/2020/03/the-key-to-inclusive-leadership

Boyatzis, R., Smith, M.L., & Van Oosten, E. (2019). *Helping people change: Coaching with compassion for lifelong learning and growth*. Harvard Business Review Press.

France, S. (2022, 25 January). The 'SixEss' threat/reward model. *Executive Support Magazine*. https://executivesupportmagazine.com/the-sixess-threat-reward-model/

Rock, D. (2008). SCARF: A brain-based model for collaborating with and influencing others. *Neuroleadership Journal, 1*. https://schoolguide.casel.org/uploads/sites/2/2018/12/SCARF-NeuroleadershipArticle.pdf

Seligman, M. (2011). *Flourish: A new understanding of happiness and wellbeing. The practical guide to using positive psychology to make you happier and healthier*. Nicholas Brealey.

6

HOW DO I MANAGE IN LIMITED TIME?

The tired brain: the enemy of effective leadership

This is one of the two questions about leading that I get asked most (the other is how to instil a sense of responsibility so that people do as they are asked, see Chapter 14). In today's world of work where we are instantly accessible, where we are constantly bombarded by information and others asking us to do things, it's difficult to be well organised, to be able to give others, and ourselves the time we need. This chapter looks at what's going on neurobiologically, as enabling our brains to work well under such pressure is crucial. If we don't manage our time well, then all the great leadership learning we do won't work. This chapter is my personal take on how to manage with the limited time that we have, enabling us to lead effectively and have time for the rest of our lives.

I believe that time is the enemy of effective leadership, as not having time to get your PFC working well undermines effective leadership. It's what my clients tell me is their biggest barrier. All the good development learned in leadership programmes or coaching can quickly be undone if there's not enough time for reflection, proper thinking and intentional practice – the time to decide how we are going to approach something.

The World Health Organization (2019) recently elevated the importance of managing time at work: it describes the impact of not attending to our time and task management at work and the burnout that can occur, as an 'occupational phenomenon' that stems directly from our collective crisis of workplace stress. The eminent psychologist and professor of Behavioural Neuroscience, Daniel Levitin, begins his well-known book, *The Organized Mind* (2015), with 'in a world of information overload our brains get very tired'.

Yet, when I did a literature survey recently, I found that there is no 'magic' to dealing with time. It's all about the maths. I found that those people who are good with time have done the sums, they know how long each task will take them and have budgeted time accordingly. In addition, over and over, studies show that those who are most organised are the most productive.

DOI: 10.4324/9781003623250-8

From my review, I think there are six key actions that we can take to manage time and be organised:

1. *Be uninterrupted*: we need energy to make the PFC work most efficiently. It takes more energy to multi-task, where we shift attention from one task to another: too much variation and multi-tasking disrupts sustained thought. So, concentrate on one thing at a time. In the human processing lab at Vanderbilt University, Dux et al (2006) observed that doing two tasks at once actually takes 30% longer and, at Microsoft, Iqbal and Horovitz (2007) demonstrated that after being interrupted by an email or a WhatsApp, it takes 15 mins to fully re-engage the PFC to think properly. So not trying to communicate while we've got one eye on our devices also becomes key

2. *Chunking*: we need to do things in a proper workable order. We need to access the temporal lobes as we're checking how we've sequenced similar things before and the hippocampus to see whether the planned sequence will work or be realistic. These feed into the PFC to be integrated. It's best to concentrate on one chunk at a time, get it done, then do the next chunk: plus, chunks are also easier to remember. It's even better if you reward yourself for each chunk completed as this creates dopamine, decreasing limbic system interference

3. *Detailed planning methods* is a well proved time and task management method. In 2023, Clockify, the online time management platform found that 83% of people don't have a dedicated time management system. Daniel Levitin dedicated whole chapters of his book *The Organized Mind* (2015) to demonstrate how the most successful people have some form of system that helps them to be organised. Most common is the Monday morning list for the week, followed by daily prioritising, although in some roles, reprioritisation needs to take place more than once a day. There are many versions of these and many online tools to help

4. *Budgeting or 'doing the maths'* is a common planning method too. I like the work of Elizabeth Saunders (2019), in which she says 'do the maths as if you are doing your finances'. She talks about evaluating the fact-based aspects of your schedule. You start with knowing how many hours you have and work out how long everything actually takes. Thus, you have a time budget, in the same way as you have a finance budget – you literally look at how much everything costs in time. Then, like a budget, you make cuts: the most effective cuts, as I've already described, are the mult-itasking ones, where we're actually wasting time or dealing with the impact of interruptions

5. *Reviewing Purpose*: one of the key reasons we get so busy is we allow our schedules to be filled with things that don't have long-term or immediate purpose. The idea here is to keep an eye on what you are doing, taking out what isn't purposeful
6. *Treat time as a systems issue.* Finally, I think that time isn't just a personal issue, it's a systems issue. Leaders have a great deal of influence over the way a team, or the whole organisation, uses its time. In an article by Jennifer Moss (2019) that I think is an important prompt, she suggests that the responsibility for creating time is not with an individual but the whole system. It is, therefore, the system, the collective responsibility of everyone involved, to address how we use time wisely and build a preventative burn-out strategy

For example, take a look at your meetings: is it possible for your team to use a purpose driven system for team meetings, where every section of the meeting has a specified purpose, which then translates into who needs to be there and do what? So many elements of meetings have a purpose that someone is not needed for. Or try for simpler solutions that are more time efficient, such as the 40 or 50 minute meetings or the standing up check in: all last less time and have been found to be equally successful – it seems a meeting takes however long the time allotted is.

I like to use Erich Dierdorff's (2020) three-factor model when helping clients with their time and task management because, in his research at DePaul University, Chicago, he found that only attending to the scheduling and planning described above, ignores two thirds of the competence needed to effectively manage time. These are:

1. *Awareness skills*: understanding how we use and think about time.
   Dierdorff demonstrated that people are not at all accurate in self-evaluating their time management proficiency. He suggests we have an acute lack of accurate self-awareness. For example, we cannot tell when our tired, limbic system overloaded brain is causing our analytic systems in our PFC to be impaired. We don't notice when a range of time biases creep in, including task completion bias where we do the easy tasks first, not attempting and delaying the harder ones, which creates a false sense of security. Or, we fall into the 'planning fallacy' where we are overly optimistic about how long something will take and what unanticipated event may crop up and get in the way.
   Only when we realise how we are approaching our use of time and what happens to us when we have a tired brain (in other words, enter the threat state), can we work out what solutions will work best for us, as we need to match the arrangement skills to what we find hard

2. *Arrangement skills*: how we design and organise goals, plans, schedules and tasks. Most of my 1–6 actions above are arrangement skills. While these are very important, they don't work well unless we attend to *why* we struggle with time, our awareness skills, and then habitualise our chosen tools, otherwise they don't work. These rely on our …

3. *Adaptation skills*: how we habitualise any tools and mechanisms. There are a number of methods of habitual change – I've borrowed and adapted this one from James Clear (2018). This has four steps:

   - *Have a desire for change*: there needs to be a good purpose in place for a change in habit or using a new tool or process. This needs to be rewarding in that when you visualise using the new habit, it brings you something needed, attractive or preferred. We are enhancing our dopamine mechanisms here, anticipating feelings of pleasure to motivate us to repeat the action
   - *Have a clear, easy trigger*: we need an immediate reminder to use the new way. We need cues that are obvious, so that we can use the new way easily. If it's too hard, it begins to create a threat state. This could be a colour-coding system or some other way of making something noticeable so that we don't forget to use it: Clear suggests putting your gym bag somewhere obvious to remind you to go to the gym. This is a highly intentional action, knowing in advance that we are going to respond in this new way, at this moment, means we are more likely to carry out this new behaviour
   - *Make the response easy*: whatever we need to change needs to be easy in the first instance. Perhaps we'll spend just two minutes on it to start with; we can begin with a simple system and gradually make it more complex. Habit stacking helps here: this is where we add a new habit to one we already have. Perhaps you already have a Monday morning priority setting of 10 minutes – you could add a maths activity to calculate how long those three biggest tasks will take
   - *Build in reward*: this is the enjoyment, the satisfaction of having taken some action. It's noticing the impact of the new action and being satisfied we've done it that helps us to repeat and do it again. This is where that dopamine hit comes in, if we don't notice this moment, the new habit is less likely to stick

6.1 Self-reflection

- What do you do already to manage time and task? Congratulate yourself on these. Can you extend any of these actions?

- Where do you struggle? Analyse this and what happens to you. Spend some time on building your awareness of how you use time before you try to move to solutions/arrangement techniques
- What could you do to build on your effective time and task management techniques?
- Could you work with others to address this systemically? Is there something in your joint system that could make a difference if you all embraced it together?
- When you've decided on what you may do differently, consider how to habitualise this, otherwise its less likely to stick

References

Clear, J. (2018). *Atomic habits: The easy and proven way to build good habits and break bad ones.* Penguin.

Clockify (2023). Workplace productivity statistics for 2023 (and beyond). https://clockify.me/productivity-statistics

Dierdorff, E.C. (2020, 29 January). Time management is about more than life hacks. *Harvard Business Review.* https://hbr.org/2020/01/time-management-is-about-more-than-life-hacks

Dux, P.E., Ivanhoff, J., Asplund, C.L., & Maroia, R. (2006). Isolation of a central bottleneck of information processing with time-resolved fMRI. *Neuron 52*(6) 1109–1120.

Iqbal, S.T. & Horovitz (2007). Disruption and recovery of computing tasks: field study analysis and directions. Paper presented at the Proceedings of the SIGCHI Conference on Human Factors in Computing Systems, San Jose, California.

Levitin, D. (2015). *The organized mind: The science of preventing overload, increasing productivity and restoring your focus.* Penguin.

Moss, J. (2019, 11 December). Burnout is about your workplace, not your people. *Harvard Business Review.* https://hbr.org/2019/12/burnout-is-about-your-workplace-not-your-people

Saunders, E.G. (2019). Stop work overload by setting these boundaries: Create a time budget and reclaim your life. In S.D. Friedman, E.G. Saunders, P. Bregman, & D.W. Dowling (Eds), *HBR guide to work–life balance.* Harvard Business Review Press.

World Health Organization (2019, 28 May). Burn-out an "occupational phenomenon". *International Classification of Diseases.* https://www.who.int/news/item/28-05-2019-burn-out-an-occupational-phenomenon-international-classification-of-diseases

7

HOW DO I ENGAGE AND MOTIVATE A SET OF DIVERSE PEOPLE WITH DIFFERENT VIEWS?

The neurobiology of inclusion and psychological safety

This chapter presents a practical view of a very important contemporary topic. There's much happening in the brain that's relevant to inclusion: primarily, that threat states are created by any form of exclusion experienced, for example, when we are not heard or included, when we believe we are treated unfairly or discriminated against. Any form of exclusion experienced in our teams means that we are being highly ineffective leaders. This chapter summarises what I think leaders can do to be highly inclusive leaders. First, I make the case for being an inclusive leader. I consider the impact of exclusion and why it occurs, looking at the neurobiology of unconscious bias and how to be aware of and overcome this. This takes me to psychological safety, creating the conditions that enable people to thrive. I look first at what psychological safety really is, then spend time considering what leaders can realistically do to increase this in teams and organisations.

7.1 Inclusion

There are specialist courses these days offering inclusive leadership. According to Bourke and Titus (2020), two of the most prominent voices in this field, there are six needed traits of a truly inclusive leader:

1. *Visible commitment*: they commit to diversity, model inclusive behaviour, ensuring they hold others accountable: they champion inclusion
2. *Humility and courage*: highly inclusive leaders speak up and challenge the status quo. They look for and confront exclusion and unfairness. They are humble about their strengths and weaknesses
3. *Awareness of bias*: an inclusive leader is able to show awareness of personal blind spots, of system flaws, and is willing to achieve a meritocracy

DOI: 10.4324/9781003623250-9

4. *Curiosity about others*: they demonstrate an open mindset, have a deep curiosity about others, are willing and able to listen without judging, using empathy to understand others
5. *Cultural intelligence*: inclusive leaders are interested in, observant and respectful, of other cultures
6. *Effective collaboration*: these leaders are willing to empower others, alert to diverse perspectives and psychological safety, and have team cohesion as an action

In this list of leadership behaviours, the commitment to being inclusive is thought to be the most important as it provides the mindset that will assist with attaining the other five. In Bourke and Titus's research studies, they demonstrated that when a leader was properly inclusive there was a 17% increase in performance levels, including enhanced high-quality decision making, teams demonstrated a 29% increase in collaborative behaviour and there was a 10% improvement in the perception of inclusion that, in turn, led to work attendance increasing by close to one day a year per employee.

It's been well documented that not attending to inclusion and diversity affects well-being, decreases performance, increases attrition, creating pay gaps and inequity that potentially result in legal costs and settlements. Exclusion, the opposite of what is being described in this chapter, creates very unhappy, disengaged, angry employees. The UK Chartered Institute of Personnel and Development (CIPD) said 'the ethical case for building diverse organisations is indisputable' (2021). They define inclusion as 'when people feel valued and accepted in their team and in the wider organisation, without having to conform'. Furthermore, 'inclusive organisations support employees, regardless of their background or circumstance, to thrive at work. To do this, they need to have practices and processes in place to break down barriers to inclusion, and, importantly, they need to value difference' (CIPD, 2019).

7.2 Exclusion

Exclusion creates a threat state, a strong one. Since the brain reacts to social threat, any form of exclusion results in a stronger than usual threat state: rejection, loneliness and loss of attachments are strongly felt emotional states, often embodied, leading to physical responses. Exclusion threats are created when we are not heard or included, when we believe we are treated unfairly or discriminated against.

Specific behaviours that we experience when we are excluded are characterised by decreased pro-social behaviours including withdrawal, an increased perception of unfairness, in group and out group behaviours, where groups polarise, and decreased self-regulation, most likely for the angry range of behaviours, and increased hypervigilance, where someone is more likely to see and experience microaggressions. When excluded we are more likely to be perceiving and responding using the ineffective ego states.

Anyone who has experienced any form of exclusion in the past will experience this even more strongly as similar experiences in our memory banks will be activated. This can leave you hypersensitive to similar threats. Previous trauma means that in a similar situation the PFC hijack is more profound, so strong that freeze mechanisms set in, with immobility and the inability to speak being common reactions. Emotional responses may be dysregulated with fear and anger mechanisms particularly affected, meaning there are likely to be very strong reactions.

7.2.1 Unconscious bias

When we look at why humans exclude others, there are a range of judgements behind these behaviours, from racism to sexism through to common biases such as the halo bias, where we are more likely to gravitate towards, and be influenced by, people we see as beautiful or clever. Googling different biases leads to 10–12 different types of bias: neuroscientists at the Neuroleadership Institute identified 150 and then distilled this into five categories that they call the SEEDS model (Lieberman et al., 2015).

SEEDS model: 150 biases categorised into five

1. Similarity: people like me better than others
2. Expedience: it feels right so it must be true
3. Experience: my perception/history tells me this is true
4. Distance: close is better than far, so I chose something near to me to experience
5. Safety: safe is better than going out on a limb

Lieberman et al. (2015)

Unconscious bias is what the brain does even more of when it is dominated by the limbic system: bias is fast, automatic thinking, where there is no checking for evidence, where there's little to no PFC activity. There is no place for such judgemental (Critical Parent) and biased behaviour in the workplace, or elsewhere. However, this is how our brain naturally operates, so we have to work extra hard to be aware of when we are biased, know which biases we are most likely to enact and be open to others pointing out when our actions are, or are perceived to be, biased. This requires us to work even harder to attain reward states for ourselves and others. In a reward state, when the PFC is accessible, we are more likely to be able to spot our own bias, to test these for evidence and to be able, consciously to choose those effective inclusive, leadership behaviours referred to at the start of this chapter and in Chapter 2 describing the effective ego states

7.3 Decreasing biased thinking and behaviour

Methods of increasing conscious thought and self-assessing for bias include:

1. *SNLF*: slow, notice, listen and reflect: a reflective practice activity useful for increasing self-awareness. Here we create space to slow down, where we can engage in a mindful moment focusing on how we're feeling, what we've said, what we've heard and how we've reacted to what others have said. Through this reflective activity we bring our unconscious thoughts to conscious awareness and are able to check our and behaviour for bias
2. *Intentional practice* activities where we carefully plan and rehearse what we're going to say to have optimal impact (see Jennifer Porter's (2019) international preparation method, in Chapter 13). If we are aware of our potential bias this is a good way of overcoming those ineffective, automatic actions, increasing the opportunities for reward conditions for others and ourselves
3. *Any action that manages and regulates limbic system activity* (see Chapter 4 that covers how to keep the brain in a 'reward' state)
4. *Going back to purpose*, particularly personal purpose. Being clear with yourself and then explaining to others what your intentions are

7.4 Psychological safety

What I'm referring to here is known as creating 'psychological safety', which is an environment where people can be heard, understood and be their authentic selves. This is a highly desirable atmosphere expected by many in today's workplaces. Leadership behaviours that create psychological safety include a list that you will be familiar with from previous chapters: curiosity, care, compassion, listening, understanding, honesty, collaboration, recognition, being given information and choice – all reward enhancing, effective ego states. These stimulate oxytocin and dopamine and are essential behaviours to increase inclusion. Mary-Frances Winters (2014) is another prominent voice in the inclusive leadership world: in her model, six out of nine characteristics of effective inclusive leaders demonstrate these behaviours, including the ability to modify listening skills, asking necessary and appropriate questions, the ability to manage conflict constructively, to show respect and interest in other people and to strive to interact meaningfully with those who you perceive as different.

I think that psychological safety is a misunderstood concept: Amy Edmondson (2019), who coined the term and concept, defines this as 'the belief that one will not be punished or humiliated for speaking up with ideas, questions, concerns, or mistakes'. In order to do this an environment of reward states needs to be created, otherwise the response will be the opposite, as a leader speaking about mistakes or concerns can be inherently threatening. One way of creating psychological safety is to provide comfort and reassurance, which, done in the absence of tough feedback, is likely to lead to an avoidance of innovation and risk, where the majority stay silent as comfort and cohesion are preferred over threat. True psychological safety and, indeed, being an inclusive leader, means being prepared for, and expecting, uncomfortable feelings, often not being liked. It requires toleration of the discomfort that transparency brings.

So, how do we create environments that are truly psychologically safe? In small steps is the usual answer: this is not about suddenly expecting everyone to be wholly open and honest from the get-go or just because there's a team event coming up, it's more about building trust over a period of time.

7.5 Growing psychological safety to support inclusion

As the literature on building psychological safety grows – there are more and more emerging examples of how to achieve this – here are some of my favourites:

- Have 'blooper' (failure) of the week in every team meeting: this way talking about failure and learning from it becomes an acceptable norm
- Systematise the difficult conversations so that they stop being difficult, deliberately have one difficult team conversation every team meeting. Set up boundaries and norms for how everyone is to behave. This helps to desensitise team discomfort
- Appoint everyone in your team 'accountability managers': it becomes everyone's duty to spot bias, gently and sensitively pointing it out to the individual responsible
- Make an 'if... then' plan: this is where we predict what we'll do in a situation where we've noticed we react with bias to difference. I love June Sarpong's example in her book *Diversify*: she didn't like tattoos; on meeting someone covered in tattoos she remembered her 'if ... then'. She remembered to be curious and to engage the person instead of backing off and ignoring them
- Making sure that not all meetings with your team are task focused. Build in unstructured, getting to know each other time with the focus on inquiring about the others' needs and experiences

- In team sessions ask 'what am I/are we missing'?'This is a question routinely asked to avoid confirmation bias and to enable those who have been quiet or uncomfortable to speak up
- Practice humility, being comfortable with saying 'I don't have the answers' or 'I was wrong'

Through these types of activities, Amy Edmondson demonstrates that 'here, learning and inclusion happens'. There are many more examples in her book, *The Fearless Organization* (2019) and in Helbig and Norman's very practical book, *The Psychological Safety Handbook* (2003).

7.6 How to create inclusion the neuroscience way

In summary, there are thought to be four key ways to create inclusion the neuroscience way:

1. *Decrease threat*: inclusive leaders are focused on decreasing threats for themselves and others and building reward state environments
2. *Be aware of your own impact*: look inwards, recognise potential threats that you may pose, recognise your ineffective ego state behaviours or those that may be perceived as a threat to others. Know that your intent doesn't always equal your impact
3. *Work extra hard* to create inclusive, 'safe' teams and organisations: use all the effective ego states. Build oxytocin stimulating situations. Watch for ineffective ego state responses in case you have inadvertently created threat
4. *Create habits* to decrease threat and increase good quality thinking and behaviour in the system. Regularly engage in team activities, such as the ones above, that celebrate diversity, allow for honest conversations and for failure to be discussed. This way, you and your team gradually become habituated to discomfort

7.7 Self-refection

- Take a look at the six traits of inclusive leadership, how inclusive do you think you really are?
- Do you recognise exclusion for yourself or anyone you work with?
- Are you aware of your common biases? Google the most common 12 biases and honestly consider whether any of these apply to you

- Deliberately ask someone to be your unconscious bias accountability manager alerting you to when you demonstrate your biases
- How psychologically safe are the teams you are a member of? Consider the team that you manage: how safe do members feel? How could you enhance psychological safety in your team?
- Do you engage in any of the activities above designed to grow psychological safety (or any others you've come across elsewhere)? If not, which one could you regularly adopt?

References

Chartered Institute of Personnel and Development (2019, 23 September). *Building inclusive workplaces: Assessing the evidence on workplace inclusion.* https://www.cipd.org/uk/knowledge/evidence-reviews/building-inclusive-workplaces/

Chartered Institute of Personnel and Development (2021, 1 October). *Beyond diversity training: What works in making workplaces more inclusive?* https://www.cipd.org/uk/views-and-insights/thought-leadership/the-world-of-work/eliminating-prejudice-workplace/

Edmondson, A.C. (2019.) *The fearless organization: Creating psychological safety in the workplace for learning, innovation and growth.* Wiley.

Helbig, K., & Norman, M. (2023). *The psychological safety playbook: Lead more powerfully by being more human.* Page Two Press.

Lieberman, M.D., Rock, D., Grant, H., & Cox. C. (2015, November). Breaking bias updated: the SEEDS® model. *NeuroLeadership Journal, 6.* https://neuroleadership.co.in/portfolio-items/breaking-bias-updated-the-seeds-model-2/

Porter, J. (2019, 19 June). How to move from self-awareness to self-improvement. *Harvard Business Review.* Available at https://hbr.org/2019/06/how-to-move-from-self-awareness-to-self-improvement.

Sarpong, J. (2017). *Diversify: Six degrees of integration.* HQ.

Winters, M.F. (2014). From diversity to inclusion: An inclusion equation. In B.M. Ferdman & B.R. Deane (Eds.), *Diversity at work: The practice of inclusion* (pp. 205–228). Jossey-Bass. doi.org/10.1002/9781118764282.ch7

Section III

COMMUNICATION: USING THE EGO STATES

In this section I show how to use the ego state model (Chapter 2), by applying this to understanding and changing difficult relationship dynamics (Chapter 8), and showing how to use effective ego states to better handle disagreements (or how to get out of the conflict loop) (Chapter 9). Chapter 10 brings two base models together, showing how to use the effective ego states to create reward states (see Chapter 1). In Chapter 8, I also introduce another concept from Transactional Analysis, the Strokes, which are units of recognition. I look at how very simple acts of validation, recognition and affirmation enhance relationships.

DOI: 10.4324/9781003623250-10

8

WHAT'S GOING WRONG IN THIS WORKPLACE RELATIONSHIP?

Using the ego states to understand relationship dynamics

Ego states is an easy to use concept for enhancing relationships. With small tweaks to our own behaviours we can invite very different responses from others. At the end of Chapter 2 it was sounding very easy, just decrease the ineffective and increase the effective ego states. It's actually more nuanced that that. In this chapter I show you how to use each of the effective ego states well; the secret is to rely on all three of the effective ones, especially in the most difficult situations. I also show you how to use each effective ego state well and to grow the one, or two, that you use least.

8.1 Overplayed ego states

So far, the message has been that to create and enhance effective relationships we simply need to stay effective and decrease the ineffective ego states. Of course, it's not quite as simple that. We can overuse the effective ego states where the inadvertent impact is that our good intent is perceived as threat. In the sections below I'm looking at how this happens and what to do to balance the use of the effective ego states to have optimal impact.

8.1.1 Overplayed Adult

You may be a naturally logical person whose preferred style of communication is to swap and gain facts and data; if so, you'll be operating primarily in the Adult ego state. That's great – you'll be skilled at working things through and information giving. This style of communication will work very well with others who also operate primarily using their Adult ego state. However, too much use of the Adult ego state can be an overplayed strength: your skills in rational argument may be perceived by someone as a threat, as you may come across as intimidating to someone who isn't as skilled at being in Adult as you are. Your body language when you are concentrating in Adult may look cold or fierce to others or you may impart too much information at once, overwhelming people. To others you may seem monotonous, as some

DOI:10.4324/9781003623250-11

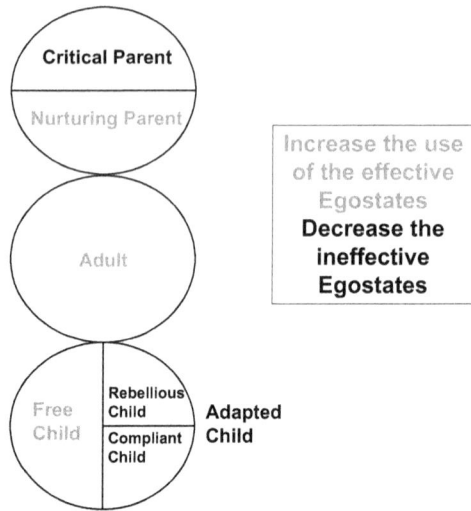

Figure 8.1 Effective and ineffective ego states

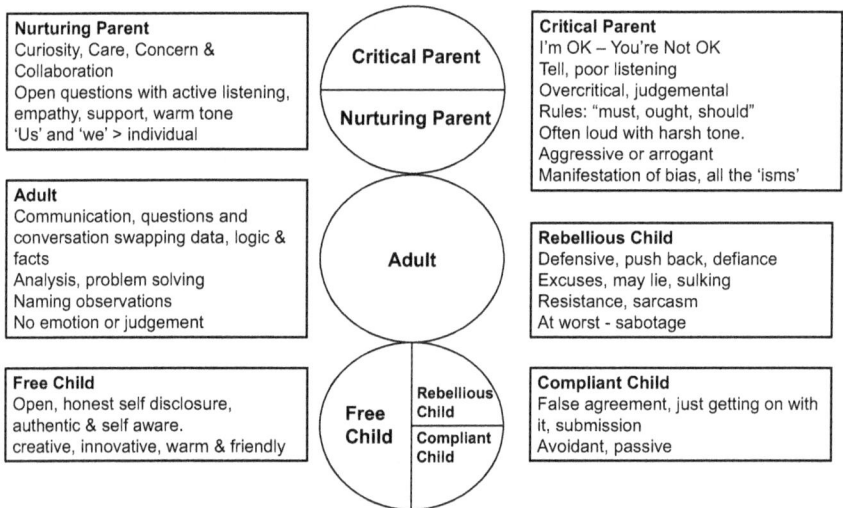

Figure 8.2 Communication from the six ego states

people with a well-developed Adult ego state don't use enough intonation in their voice and their delivery can be flat.

In all these scenarios, your reciprocal impact may not be Adult–Adult as you expect: you have a good chance at being perceived as Critical Parent, as you may be unintentionally having an intimidating, forceful or overwhelming impact. Your focused body language or fact-heavy style of delivery can be hard to hear for these who aren't naturally Adult; they are more likely to receive you as arrogant, not caring or unempathetic.

The reciprocal responses you get back may confuse you: typical 'crossed transactions', ones that aren't what we expect in a particular scenario, may be:

- Compliant Child, characterised by minimal engagement and quick agreement, the submissive stance, where you often don't get back much interest, what you ask for or the other doesn't carry out your expectation
- Rebellious Child, common when others perceive that the interaction is imbalanced, where you have more air space, have brought too much information or they have been overwhelmed. Here you may encounter defensive reactions or even anger that surprises you. This is often where misunderstandings begin: one person gives a purely Adult explanation that is misheard or misunderstood because of the use of a single ego state and the other reacts negatively
- Critical Parent, where the other will judge your facts or your narrative. Here you may receive criticism and judgement in response or be dismissed

If you recognise these descriptions, it's important to use more Nurturing Parent and Free Child in your communication, to 'grow' the effective ego states you are not using so much of, especially with people whose natural style isn't as Adult as yours. Don't shrink your Adult though: it's a key strength, a fundamental part of your talent and what makes you effective. The development action here is to make that Adult ego state work better. We do this by using the three effective ego states in tandem.

8.1.2 Overplayed Nurturing Parent

I meet an incredibly high number of leaders who have chosen leadership as a means of helping others. They are concerned for their colleagues, their service users or customers, they are interested in them and give their time willingly, often with open door policies. They are warm, caring people who gladly offer their support. They have a strong Nurturing Parent ego state with great intent. And yet, they often receive feedback that they lack impact, they are almost always short of time and I note they are the first to struggle with their own resilience. Their direct reports rely on them to solve their problems and sometimes they feel taken advantage of. This is a description of the Nurturing Parent ego state being used too much.

The reciprocal responses to Nurturing Parent are care and concern back, with more Nurturing Parent, or Free Child, where others open up in response. Someone with a large Nurturing Parent is, therefore, a trusted colleague: they create psychological safety and cohesive teams, people feel heard, they are well liked. All great leadership attributes to be encouraged. However, if they do this too much, they don't always get the responses they expect or the performance they need.

Sometimes the big Nurturing Parent is too empathic, they do too much for someone, inadvertently disempowering them. This style of leadership does not lead to a solutions culture – it's the leader here who is providing most of the solutions. They actually experience annoyance or criticism back, Critical Parent or Rebellious Child, that comes as a surprise. This phenomenon can be best explained by another concept from TA, a 'drama triangle', originally described by Karpman (1968). It works like this:

1.   The Nurturing Parent leader wants to help, this helpful attitude isn't perceived as an effective ego state. Instead, it's seen as interfering, patronising or disempowering

2.   Characteristically, there's an initial Compliant Child response. This may seem odd because it's hard to be angry directly with someone who is so nice. You will be a trusted person to whom others turn, so the response is one of 'yes, you're right' For that person, their emotions may be out of control, conflicted and/or unhappy. There's also a sense of 'poor me', of helplessness: this is known as the 'Victim Position'

3.   At some point there's an emotional flick to Rebellious Child, instead of ongoing submissive behaviour, the resentment and annoyance becomes too great. Now that lovely Nurturing Parent is on the receiving end of defensiveness, push back and resistance. It's very confusing. Worse, the other begins to negatively judge their leader, to see them as weak or ineffectual. These Critical Parent behaviours are hurtful to the leader, trust

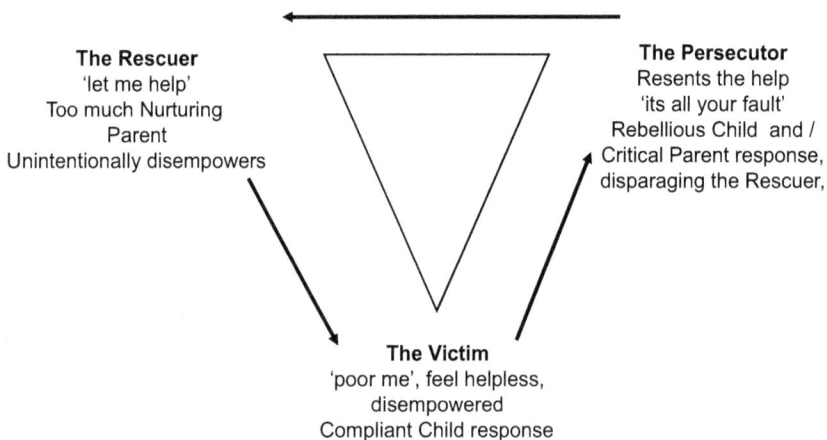

The Rescuer
'let me help'
Too much Nurturing
Parent
Unintentionally disempowers

The Persecutor
Resents the help
'its all your fault'
Rebellious Child and /
Critical Parent response,
disparaging the Rescuer,

The Victim
'poor me', feel helpless,
disempowered
Compliant Child response

Figure 8.3 A drama triangle

is diminished, relationships are now breaking down. This is known in a Drama Triangle as the 'Persecutor Position'

This situation has arisen as the Nurturing Parent ego state is being used too much. What mitigates is more use of the Adult, the more factual ego state that gives more clarity and sets stronger expectations, as well as some use of the Free Child, especially more description of why you want someone to do something. More on how to do this in Chapter 9.

My leadership development and coaching work is quite split between those people I encourage to be more Nurturing Parent and those whom I want to support using their great caring and compassionate characteristics more effectively (by encouraging them to use their Adult and Free Child more confidently and clearly). These big Nurturing Parents find themselves taken for granted, not achieving their team's objectives and confused about their leadership style.

8.1.3 Overplayed Free Child

The overplayed Free Child is characterised by too much sharing, showing voluntary vulnerability too much, excessive levity or ideas. They come across as flimsy, needy or with little depth, often changing their minds. They are easily judged, often gossiped about, dismissed as a serious contender and frequently ignored. They are the subject of others' Critical Parent judgement. This also applies to those who care deeply, who demonstrate great passion but who are judged as 'activists' and find that their heartfelt message isn't taken seriously.

In the TA model, the path to higher effectiveness for the naturally Free Child is to increase the amount of Adult and Nurturing Parent communication. In particular Adult is most useful, as this balances the emotion and the passion with the facts, data, logic and expectation messages. The Adult brings a calm, concise delivery style that acts as a counterpoint to the emotional message. Adding in some time to properly hear the information the other brings as well can lead to both parties spending more time together in Adult to decide where to go with what is important to the Free Child, thereby giving more weight to what they so keenly want to invest in. Ending up in Adult, being solutions and future focused, is a key communication transaction that I'll explore more in Chapter 9.

8.2 Development where there's an overplayed ego state

If you recognise that you have an overplayed ego state here's some key guidance for your development:

1. Never try to shrink a big effective ego state. It is the state that represents your leadership strengths, it will be what you are respected for most. Being in this state will allow you to communicate from your reward states
2. To balance the impact of that big state, grow one or both of the other two effective ego states. Introduce more curiosity, listening and care from Nurturing Parent and/or be more honest about what's going on for you, what you need from Free Child
3. This is not about having the three effective ego states in balance, although this would have an optimal impact if you do; it's about balancing the impact of a big effective ego state with one or both of the others to help you to be even more effective

8.3 How conflict loops play out at work

A conflict loop is a set of reciprocal transactions played out entirely in the ineffective ego states. In their pure form they are the repetition of two ego states between two people, criticism and negative judgement from Critical Parent and defensiveness and resistance from Rebellious Child. They are highly dysfunctional, neither party is properly listening to the other, both are likely to be feeling angry and hurt, prefrontal cortex deep thinking is certainly not occurring, biases and poor behaviour abound. These are dangerous and undermining situations for both. In the workplace, I see what I think of as 'muted' Rebellious Child reactions in conflict loops, as pure Rebellious Child is career limiting. To say what you really want in an unchecked angry way is the path to the front door.

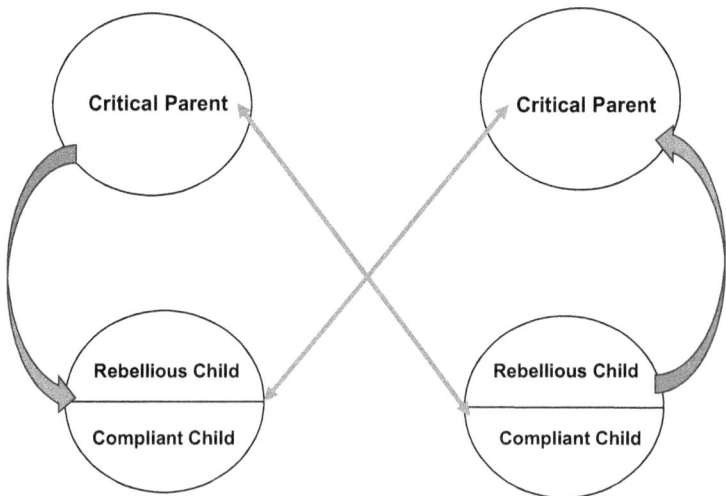

Figure 8.4 The conflict loop

Conflict loops can occur as one-offs or patterns that two individuals slip into every time they meet, in such cases there will have been repeated disagreement over a period of time. Trust is poor, suspicion is high. Knowing that you are meeting with the person you are in a prolonged conflict loop with will keep you up at night rehearsing what you are going to say, or afterwards going over what you wished you'd said and how you'll deal with them next time.

These are the relationships that we dread, the ones that may ultimately cause us to leave an organisation. The ones as leaders we need to sort out and mediate between team members or peers. They are deeply uncomfortable states of threat that affect our performance at work. They are best avoided and carefully managed as, once embedded, these patterns of relationships are hard to turn around. Chapter 9 is all about how to manage conflict loops.

8.4 Self-reflection

If you have a workplace relationship that's not working very well, consider the following:

- What is the effective ego state that you use most?
- What impact does this have?
- With that person, could you grow and use another effective ego state to balance your strongest?
- How could you do that, what behaviours would you need to do more of?
- Are you stuck in a conflict loop with another person? What's the impact on you and on them?
- For that conflict loop, can you plot out the Critical Parent and Rebellious Child communication transactions that you are both enacting to help you to understand what is happening?

Reference

Karpman, S. (1968). Fairy tales and script drama analysis. *Transactional Analysis Bulletin*, 7(26), pp. 39–43. https://www.karpmandramatriangle.com/pdf/DramaTriangle.pdf

9

WE DISAGREE: HOW DO
I HANDLE THAT?

How to have conversations that have impact, but don't lead to conflict and disengagement

I think this is one of the hardest activities of leadership. It's inevitable that we are going to disagree with and/or be frustrated by colleagues, I certainly have. I think that how we handle those disagreements and moments of irritation so that relationships are maintained is a crucial part of the responsibility of leadership. In this chapter, I explore our communication choices: even in threat states, in the most testing of situations, it is psychologically possible to choose to remain effective, resisting the almost visceral urge to jump to the ineffective Critical Parent or Rebellious Child position. Here, I present a range of strategies to communicate effectively, even when we perceive there's a massive Critical Parent having a go at us or winding us up. There's a pot of ideas here: I urge you to 'cherry pick', choose the strategies, techniques and ways of communication that resonate for you. As you go through this chapter, pick just three to take away and try out.

When we receive an ineffective response to our attempts to convey something, when these are a surprise, unintended or when we find ourselves in conflict loops, we are not at our best: leadership is impacted, we and others are likely to be in the threat states. This chapter is all about how to use the effective ego states as much as possible even in those very challenging moments. This is a chapter about how to manage our relationships well to have the desired impact and avoid conflict and consequent disengagement.

9.1 Communication type is a choice

When I introduce my clients to the ego states I begin by saying that this model helps us to explain our communication behaviours and the impact that we have. Crucially, this model presents the choices that we have when communicating. We will often want someone else to change their behaviours, to stop being so defensive or obtuse and that's fine, it's just that the only way to change someone else's behaviours is to change our own first. It was Barack Obama who said 'change will not come if we wait for some other person or some other time. We are the ones we've been waiting for. We are the change

   DOI:10.4324/9781003623250-12

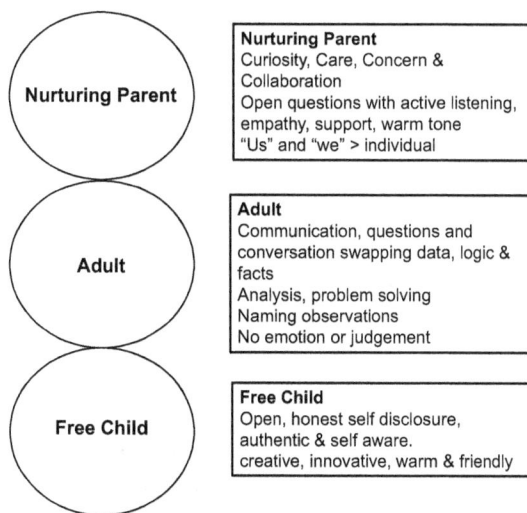

Figure 9.1 The effective ego states

that we seek' (BarackObama.com, 2008). This is considered a universal truth in psychology, demonstrated by the law of reciprocal transactions: if you offer someone a specific behaviour, there's a good chance that they will respond to you in kind, with a matching reciprocal transaction.

To help us with making effective conscious decisions are 'moments of choice' (see Figure 9.2) where we have a split second to assess our behavioural choices. This concept comes from the clinical methodology of Acceptance and Commitment Therapy (for example, see Bailey et al., 2014). I've adapted this, focusing on that moment when we can choose our behaviour. There is a moment in difficult situations, before prefrontal cortex accessibility is strongly diminished, where we can still use the analytic and empathic networks. By wisely using this moment, we can decide whether the behaviours we are about to use are an 'effective move', one that deliberately chooses an effective ego state, or an 'ineffective move', one that is either going to be deliberately provocative, or be perceived by the other as an ineffective ego state.

To help in making those choices, consider which ego state you want to do more or less of and home in on the suggestions below.

9.2 Decreasing the ineffective ego states

9.2.1 Critical Parent

Instead of 'you should, you haven't, you did or you didn't', try to use different language and tone to express your frustrations, anger or disappointments.

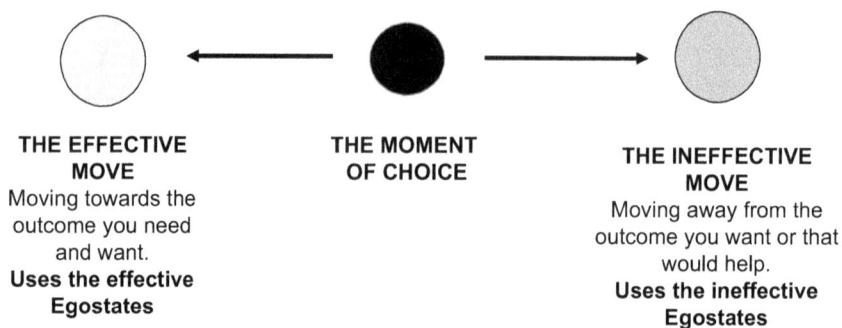

THE EFFECTIVE MOVE	THE MOMENT OF CHOICE	THE INEFFECTIVE MOVE
Moving towards the outcome you need and want. **Uses the effective Egostates**		Moving away from the outcome you want or that would help. **Uses the ineffective Egostates**

Figure 9.2 The moment of choice

You could say 'I observed', 'I believe' or 'I heard that you have done [whatever fact is relevant]'. All these statements are more obvious expressions of Adult facts.

Slow your speech down, calm your voice tone and take a physical step back.

Check for rules: instead of saying 'should or ought', say 'I expected you to do xx, I'm surprised you didn't, I'm curious as to why not'. This is a much more balanced expression of the same thing: moving from and using all the effective ego states, that sentence moved from Adult to Free Child with the final part of the sentence, Nurturing Parent.

> To avoid being perceived as Critical Parent, speak slowly and calmly with an even tone. Say 'I'm surprised to see the *xx* that you sent me, I was expecting *yy*, I'm wondering what's been happening?' Then listen to the response carefully before responding.

9.2.2 Rebellious Child

This is all about managing yourself when you are angry, anxious, frustrated and so on. The key here is to recognise how you feel and behave in a more authentic way than attacking or putting someone down. For example, instead of 'why is it always me', 'I'm not going to bother in the future', 'suit yourself' or 'don't be ridiculous', try expressing more about how you feel and why:

*   'Why is it always me' may be better expressed as 'I don't like what I'm hearing, I'm going to need some time to think about that'

78

- 'I'm not going to bother in the future' could be 'I'm cross about how that was done. It's important to me that it's done like x because of y. In future please can we discuss this before we get to this stage'
- 'Suit yourself' possibly indicates you've been undermined or exposed. Maybe cooling off before you say anything maybe your wisest move
- 'Don't be ridiculous' is something we say when we're in a conflict loop. The best way through this is to say something about your frustrations, then find out more about why someone else said this. This is moving from Free Child to Nurturing Parent communications

In all these examples the emotion is expressed more honestly and openly or managed through Free Child. Voluntary vulnerability, learning to say what's really going on for you and why is a key leadership strength and one of the actions that helps the limbic system in the brain to be calm, allowing the PFC to be accessed.

> To avoid responding in Rebellious Child, take a moment to work out why you're cross, frustrated or worried, then try to put this into words. This means you are choosing Free Child instead of Rebellious Child and you are more likely to receive an effective reciprocal response.

9.2.3 Compliant Child

Here, we learn to speak up about what's troubling us, what we aren't saying out loud. Again, learning to be voluntarily vulnerable is key. Obviously, in truly career limiting or dangerous situations this is not appropriate. In such situations it's important to think about a plan to deal with the situation: in this case you would be compliant from Adult, as it would be sensible and logical to remain silent.

A note: there are two places from which we can be compliant, the first is Compliant Child, which is an emotional response that we use to avoid perceived threat. There's also compliant Adult, where we do as we're told because that is the logical and sensible thing to do in that situation.

> To avoid a Compliant Child response, recognise the emotion driving you. If you are nervous, frustrated or sad, then work out how to put that into words, explaining your reaction and concerns. If you realise that your compliance is not emotionally based but a sensible and logical thing to do, then take that decision forward and complete the task or the request in good faith.

9.3 Increasing and balancing the blue, effective ego states

Here are some very useful methods for helping us to stay and be heard in the effective ego states:

9.3.1 Adult

- Be careful not to use judgemental or harsh language. The word 'why' can sound accusatory, there are other ways to phrase a question such as 'I'm wondering what happened?'
- As well as imparting information, make sure you pause for people to ask you questions. This stops this ego state sounding too 'tell'
- Be careful not to deliver a monologue, instead cut what you want to say into segments, layering one at a time, pausing in between for questions
- Match your audience: with a fact-liking audience Adult will work well, for a more mixed audience tell your story with more Free Child elements and variations of tone. For example, show some enthusiasm, talk about what you like and don't like about the plans or decision
- Ask factual questions and talk about your observations or experience: our observations are classed as factual in the model, as long as we say 'I observed x, y and z'
- When you do have facts to impart, it's helpful to state these conversationally: as soon as we overlay energy, anxiety, anger or even care into our language it stops sounding factual
- Offer something that works towards a solution

It's important to remember that adult language contains no emotion and no judgement, so check the way in which you are delivering.

9.3.2 Free Child

- Use personal pronouns such as 'I' or 'me' to tell your story, experience or express vulnerability. 'We' isn't a good way of communicating Free Child as from this state we are only speaking for ourselves
- Calmly talk about what's going on for you, your position, role or purpose
- Explain to people why you think or feel the way that you do. This is an important way of communicating your purpose in any given situation. For example, explain why something is urgent or why you are frustrated. You could say:
  - 'This is why I'm saying this …'
  - 'This is important for me because …'
  - 'I'm concerned about …'

- Avoid 'you make me feel', this sounds judgemental
- Give people a taste of your reaction, going on too long, using too much Free Child can be overwhelming for people. Emotional naming is often enough for us to get this across. For example: 'I was concerned because [very short explanation]' can work just as well as telling the whole drama. This brief method is an effective way of calming the limbic system, meaning that we are more likely to gain access to our PFC and be able to access our analytic networks to solve the problem at hand
- Free Child is also about lightening the tone; if you use jokes, make them inclusive, an 'in-joke' can be perceived as Critical Parent by those not in the know
- Apologise if you've done something wrong. Being honest is an important element of Free Child

9.3.3 Nurturing Parent

The essence of Nurturing Parent is to see things from the other's perspective, thus being empathic. This depends on asking good quality curious, open questions then properly listening to their responses. When you are involved in someone else's story, properly paying attention and asking supplementary questions that are directly related, then you are automatically demonstrating elements of empathy. Tips include:

- Supporting people by asking if you can help
- Understanding people's motivation, especially when they are emotionally motivated – there is always a reason for someone's emotion and behaviour
- Asking open questions followed by actively listening
- Seeking others' opinions
- Attending to their needs
- Being compassionate
- Showing warmth and care

9.4 Getting out of the conflict loop

Of all the behavioural activities needed as leaders, exiting the conflict loop is the hardest as you are already in a threat state and so is the other person. Here are some methods, all of which enable to you to use the effective ego states more, thereby receiving effective reciprocal communication back:

- Be self-aware about what is happening
- Choose to resist the urge to give back what you get – usually giving our opinions, piling in more facts or being defensive. Remembering the 'moment of choice' can be especially helpful here

THE PSYCHOLOGY OF EFFECTIVE LEADERSHIP

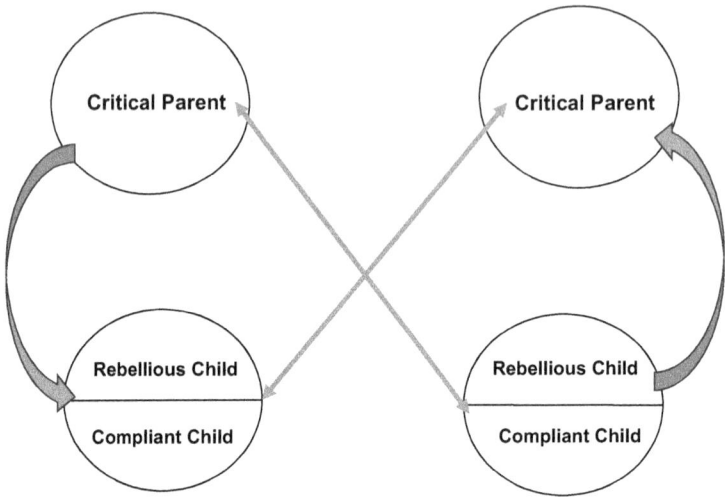

Figure 9.3 The conflict loop

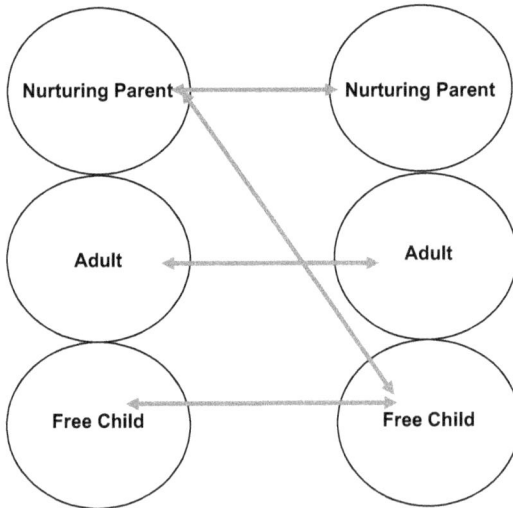

Figure 9.4 The most common effective reciprocal responses

- Instead, talk about what you believe, what you are doing and why: all these are Free Child behaviours. These show that we have good intent, where we are coming from, that we are not trying to threaten but to help
- And, most importantly, we can ask what's going on for them from Nurturing Parent and show we understand. Their intent most likely isn't to be in the red, understanding what's going on for them helps both parties to get back to an effective ego state

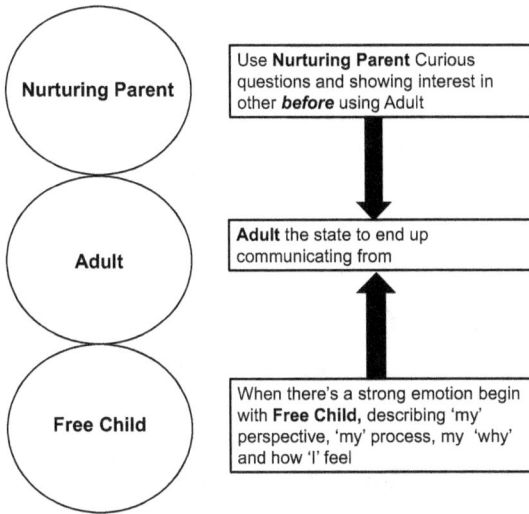

Figure 9.5 Ending up in Adult

The ideal point to get to if you've been in a conflict loop is Adult–Adult. Here, you are not blaming each other for what has happened or resisting the other's ideas. Instead, you are focused on solving whatever issue has been problematic and looking towards the future. There is a golden rule in Organisational TA: *'to end up in Adult, use Free Child or Nurturing Parent first'.* Here's how it works:

1. If you are in, or edging towards, a conflict loop, decide how strong your emotional state is. You may need to buy some time to work this out: you could ask the other a curious question while you reflect or you could take a break and arrange to reconvene in a few minutes. Once you've started to recognise conflict loops and to tune into your emotions, this step becomes easier over time

2. If your emotions are strong, start with Free Child by saying how you feel (not how the person is making you feel!). This is important, as when the other hears a clear Free Child statement, such as 'this conversation is hard for me' or 'I'm uncomfortable or disappointed about ...', there is a good chance that the reciprocal responses will be either Nurturing Parent, where they may ask you about what's going on, or Free Child, where they say what's going on for them. This is likely to lead to a very different conversation than the one characterised by a conflict loop. This model of TA suggests that either of those two exchanges are likely to lead you towards the mutual Adult to Adult position of solving a problem or working out how to go on from there

3. Alternatively, if you are not experiencing a strong emotion, or find talking about your emotions very hard, start with the Nurturing Parent. Here you really focus on what is going on for the other. You ask curious questions, listen actively and empathise. The more you ask the more this conversation naturally turns to solutions. This is not advised if you are carrying a strong emotion as then it's much harder to be properly empathic

If you've ever done this before, and you probably have without realising it, by starting in Nurturing Parent or Free Child and deepening the conversation, it naturally becomes more focused on what to do and how to move forward. Starting in Nurturing Parent or Free Child help us to get to the Adult–Adult position.

9.5 How to put this into action

In this chapter, I've really deepened the approach to using the ego states. There are a lot of suggestions here and a lot to watch out for if you are new to this. To start reflecting, ask yourself the questions below; in particular, spend some time observing your responses, especially identifying whether you have a default ineffective ego state, the one you are most likely to go to under threat. Once you are clear about this go over the notes above, pulling out specific communication strategies that you could do more or less of to have an even more effective impact. Pull out up to three small ways of communicating more effectively. Write these down, then they become easier to use next time you encounter a conflict loop.

9.6 Self-reflection

• We all have a default, ineffective ego state, the one we are most likely to go to under threat: what is yours?
• Which ego state is the one you need to either decrease or increase the most? Which three communication strategies could help you with this?
• How could you use the 'moment of choice'? Are there certain moments that you recognise where taking a few seconds could help you towards increased effectiveness or away from messing it up?
• Think about a conflict loop that you have may find yourself in, what can you do differently next time?

References

Bailey, A., Ciarrochi, J., & Harris, R. (2014). *The weight escape*. Shambhala.
BarackObamadotcom (2008, 5 February). *Barack Obama Speech: Super Tuesday* [Video]. YouTube. https://www.youtube.com/watch?v=8dzHDzvTfzQ&t=2s

10

HOW DO I GET THE BEST OUT OF MY COLLEAGUES?

Simple acts that create reward: using the ego states and introducing the 'Strokes'

If I were to pick three leadership actions that particularly make a difference, offering recognition would be one (with the other two being clear about purpose and looking beyond someone's behaviours – understanding why). This chapter is all about the psychology of recognition, why it is so important, the impact it has and how to give this authentically. Not all of us like, or are comfortable with, praise and gratitude: I often hear people say, 'I don't need recognition for doing my job'. In this chapter, I consider how we all like to give and receive differing amounts and types of reward and recognition. I provide guidance about how to authentically manage this using the effective ego states, especially when someone's recognition needs differ from ours. Fundamentally, gratitude and recognition can be strong motivators, providing all three of the key neurotransmitter substances that keep the limbic system working well. It's in our interests as leaders to make sure we are providing these for the people we lead. I demonstrate that this is not hard, there are many small ways to do this.

10.1 'OK-ness'

Eric Berne, originally a psychoanalyst, started writing about TA in the early 1960s as a way of making psychological therapies accessible to all (Berne, 1962, 1977). His central concept was one of 'OK-ness' where everyone is born OK and events in life cause us to deviate from this OK position, a concept later developed by the other well-known TA founder, Thomas Harris (1969). This of course was many years before we knew very much about the brain and way before we knew that it operated to that key principle of avoiding threat and approaching reward. These early founders of TA realised what we know today – that it's important for us to be in a state of OK-ness to behave and respond well. What they observed was that creating OK-ness isn't hard, there's a simple set of actions and communications, delivered through the effective ego states that do this by recognising another's presence. We may do this through a smile, a hug, saying 'hello', giving a compliment or

DOI:10.4324/9781003623250-13

recognising someone's value in the team. It signifies to another person that they exist and are relevant.

10.2 'Strokes'

In the TA model, any unit or type of recognition is termed a 'Stroke': each unit of recognition, used properly, is also an important way of creating reward states as we are meeting people's social needs.

Understanding how to use these simple Strokes, knowing that different people have different recognition requirements, to create

Simple everyday workplace Strokes

Eye contact
Listen
Smile
Pay attention
Ask questions
Summarise effectively
Ask more
Praise
Thank/offer gratitude
Trust with a task
Remember names
Show respect
Be honest
Help

OK-ness, enhance and maintain reward states and meet social needs is an immensely powerful tool to tailor our behaviour to others' needs. It is, perhaps, especially important in the work environment in order to engage, influence, motivate and help change others' behaviours. Particularly as, at work, we often find ourselves with colleagues who are very different from ourselves.

In a nutshell, Strokes are units of recognition that we all need to be engaged, influenced and motivated. They are simple acts to get the best from our colleagues. These calm the limbic system, creating and maintaining reward states. Strokes are not about touching anyone: recently, a number of my clients have commented that this nomenclature is outdated. The language of Strokes is still commonly used in psychotherapy, from where these models originated. I have considered changing the terminology and found this confusing and long winded. I've therefore decided to stay true to the model and language of TA. If you find the term Strokes hard, please think of these as simple acts of recognition.

10.3 Positive and negative strokes

Babies learn early on that smiling produces a positive response from people around them. This response, or positive Stroke, reinforces the behaviour and makes it more likely the baby will smile again in the future. In our interactions with others at work and in social or family situations, Strokes are the ways we acknowledge to those around us that we know they are there.

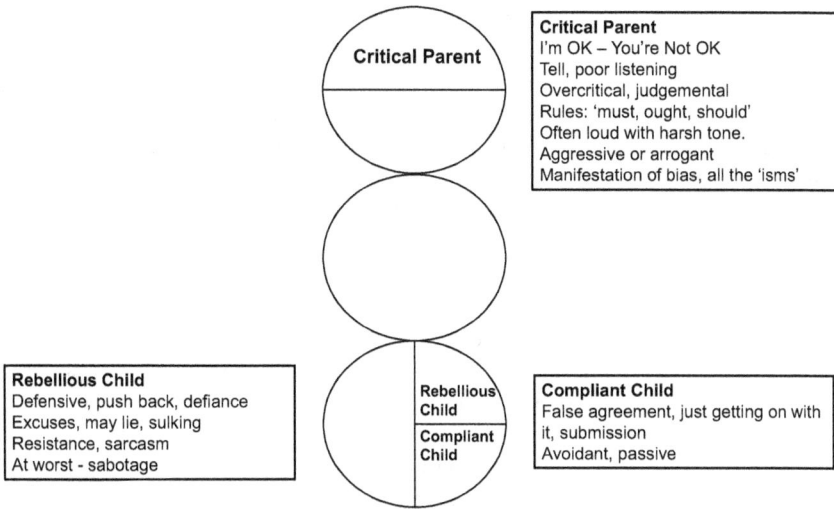

Figure 10.1 The ineffective ego states are negative Strokes

Because human beings are innately social, we all need these positive gestures of recognition. Positive Strokes include ordinary everyday politeness that we sometimes leave out when we are busy.

Without the feedback that they offer, we feel ignored, unappreciated, and ill at ease, even if we don't know exactly why. We also need to learn what not to do, so it is important that we also receive certain negative Strokes: a reprimand or information that we are doing something wrong. Without helpful negative Strokes we would not learn boundaries, understand new expectations and would continue to act in ways that are unhelpful or unproductive. Some negative Strokes are inherently critical, they are another way of describing how we convey criticism or disapproval: these are the ineffective ego states, particularly Critical Parent, and, as we'll see, these are not appropriate.

We might expect that we would always seek positive Strokes and seek to avoid negatives. This is not the case. Our need for recognition is so profound that sometimes in the absence of positive Strokes we pursue negatives, as some recognition is better than nothing.

10.4 Verbal and non-verbal strokes

Strokes can be expressed with or without language. In a work environment we deliver important positive Strokes by commenting on people's work and performance such as 'that was a good report'; 'you did really well on your presentation,' or 'thanks to everyone for getting the results in on time'. However, some of the most powerful Strokes are delivered in the absence of language. For example, looking at someone when they are talking to us is a simple positive Stroke that confirms that we are listening. Non-verbal Strokes, particularly eye contact, facial gestures and body positions, are powerful, yet simple, modes of positive Strokes.

Similarly, bringing a colleague a cup of coffee in the morning, or even just smiling in welcome are both positive Strokes. Rolling your eyes or staring at someone delivers a strong negative Stroke conveying disapproval or criticism. Walking through an office without acknowledging people could be perceived as being ignored or even dismissed. The impact of these can be huge: the way in which negative Strokes are delivered has a great impact on how they are received. A negative Stroke, delivered ineffectively, can easily be perceived as coming from Critical Parent or Rebellious Child and is likely to be responded to in kind. For example, even when the words are positive such as 'thank you for getting the statistics to me in time for the presentation', if they are delivered with an angry expression and tone of voice, the perception of a negative Stroke is likely to outweigh the positive. Negative Strokes can be unintentional as well as deliberate. The short-sighted person who has forgotten their glasses may appear to be ignoring their colleagues when they fail to return their nods of greeting!

10.5 Stroke economy: the amount of recognition

This refers to the availability, or number, of positive and negative Strokes in any given environment (or economy). We are all brought up in environments which vary in terms of the number of available Strokes: we all have different 'social needs'. Some of us were raised in highly social environments where people engaged in a lot of conversation and exchanged a lot of feedback. Others will have been brought up in environments where people were more introverted and fewer Strokes were exchanged. Because of this we all need different amounts of Strokes: we all differ in the number of Strokes that we like to give and get.

We are also the products of the wider cultural environments in which we have grown up. Understanding the different tendencies of diverse cultures is very important as this will help us to determine the number, and type, of Strokes that reflect a person's social needs.

Like individuals, different teams have different Stroke economies – you can pick up on them the minute you enter their working environment. Some places are buzzing with conversation whereas others are much quieter and more reserved.

10.6 Stroke type: different forms of recognition

We all give Strokes in different ways and people have personal preferences in terms of the type of Strokes they value. Some people are motivated by being part of a team, others by promotion. Some value money, others a career which offers a good balance between their work and home life. Day to day we differ in the type of Strokes that we like to give and get. In Chapter 5, I looked at the seven reward types; these are seven types of positive Strokes that different people need in the workplace, which range from being given clarity or a good purpose, through to hearing that they are valued, being part of a group and enabled to achieve results.

For this reason, organisations always struggle to design reward systems that work for everyone as people's preferences are so

The Seven Reward Types

Offering these are all types of positive Strokes.

1. Validation, recognition, affirmation
2. Control, agency, predictability
3. Support, acknowledgment, being heard
4. Having a good purpose
5. Belonging
6. Success, achievement, outcomes
7. Equality

different. Organisations have myriad rewards or Stroke types: the gold watch after 25 years' service; the meal out for a successful project team or the parking space when you become a senior leader. A more commonplace form of Stroke type is the exchange of food or treats in the workplace or funny jokes and personal check-ins on Team chats: these are gestures that say, 'I like you and appreciate you'. Coming from a different culture or environment that doesn't recognise this Stroke type as important can give rise to confusion.

10.7 Stroke balance: 'different strokes for different folks'

Stroke balance describes the balance between positive and negative Strokes that a person likes to receive, ultimately shaping how we all like a different number and type of Strokes to thrive. The American idiom 'different strokes for different folks' sums up this concept well. When we are growing up, we receive both positive and negative Strokes. Gradually we evolve a balance – a mixture of positive and negative Strokes with which we feel comfortable and familiar.

For example, if we have been brought up experiencing a much greater proportion of negative to positive Strokes, we are likely to develop a negative Stroke balance, seeking constructive feedback over positive Strokes. This means that, if we later find ourselves in an environment where we are exposed to a high proportion of positive Strokes, we may find it difficult to adjust, feeling overwhelmed or doubting people's authenticity. In this example it wouldn't be uncommon to be suspicious of positive Strokes.

A positive Stroke balance is the reverse of this: in this case we are likely to have grown up in environments where positive Strokes were plentiful. This means that we will try to keep a greater ratio of positives in our adult lives. We may seek out positive Strokes over negative Strokes, and we are likely to

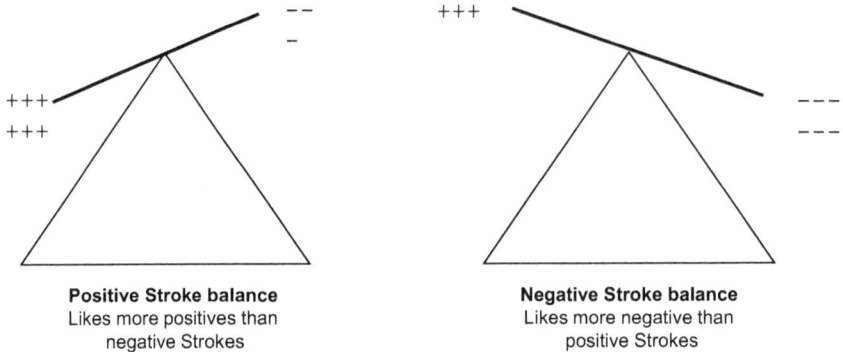

Figure 10.2 Positive and negative Stroke balances

enjoy praise and give plenty of positive Strokes to others. This does not mean we reject negative Strokes: we may prefer, and can listen better to negative Strokes when we have positive ones as well.

10.8 Getting the best from colleagues

Most of us give Strokes to others in a way that is consistent with what we look for in our own relationships, rather than what our colleagues necessarily want or need. If you're a person with a high positive Stroke balance, chances are you remember other's birthdays, say a cheery 'hello' to everyone when you come to work and provide a high economy and wide type of positive verbal and non-verbal feedback. If one of your colleagues or employees has a low positive Stroke balance, you may find this odd, maybe even irritating or offensive. In turn, you may find it difficult to understand how your frequent, enthusiastic validations can be annoying to them. In fact, these are inconsistent with their Stroke need and your colleague is experiencing your constant friendly overtures as intrusive and over-the-top. They may even question your sincerity and wonder why you can't understand that they'd rather be left alone. You may not be having the positive impact you intended.

The Golden and Platinum rules for getting the best from people

Replace the **Golden Rule**: where we give the Strokes we like to give and get ...

With the **Platinum Rule**: give the Strokes the other person needs most

In order to have a good, reciprocal relationship with a colleague or employee, it's hugely important to understand their Stroke balance, what their social need is and to try to tailor behaviour towards them. It's about being aware of the existence of varying Stroke amounts and needs, their preference for positive, negative, verbal and non-verbal Strokes. When in doubt, there's absolutely nothing wrong with asking someone how they perceive the Strokes that you are giving them. For example: 'would you like everyone at work to make a fuss about your birthday, or do you prefer to keep celebrations low-key?' or 'what sort of feedback do you find most useful when it comes to helping you continue to improve your performance at work?' That last question is one of my favorites for team sessions: asking 'how do you like to recognised and appreciated at work' is a great way of getting to know how to get the best out of each other.

10.9 Strokes and the effective ego states

Positive Strokes are small acts of recognition communicated, either verbally or non-verbally, from the effective ego states. Strokes, like any other form of communication, are reciprocal. A Free Child positive Stroke, honestly telling someone how kind you've found them is likely to be met with either their Free Child giving you an honest impression back or by their Nurturing Parent, listening to what you have to say.

As soon as there is a perception of a negative Stroke, there is the risk of this being perceived as Critical Parent and increases the likelihood that it will be met by Rebellious Child or Compliant Child responses. In the example

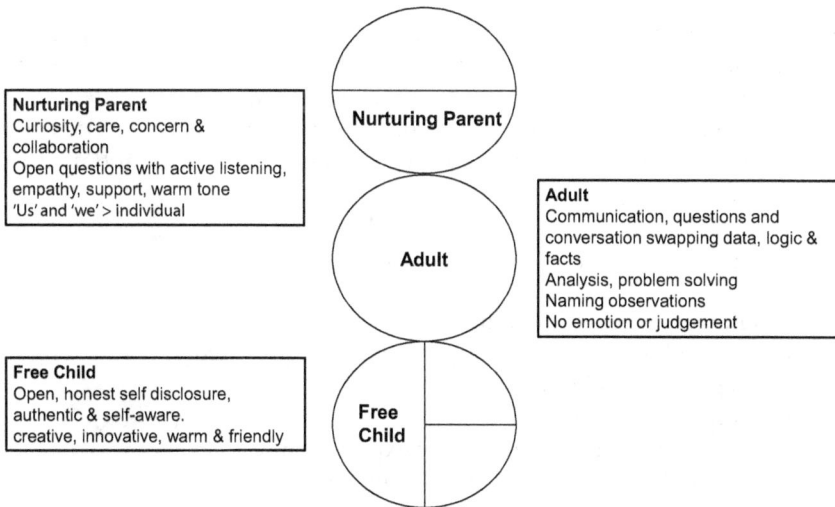

Nurturing Parent
Curiosity, care, concern & collaboration
Open questions with active listening, empathy, support, warm tone
'Us' and 'we' > individual

Adult
Communication, questions and conversation swapping data, logic & facts
Analysis, problem solving
Naming observations
No emotion or judgement

Free Child
Open, honest self disclosure, authentic & self-aware.
creative, innovative, warm & friendly

Figure 10.3 The effective ego states

above, if they perceive that you aren't being honest, there's some flaw in your narrative or you've picked the wrong sort of Stroke to give them, they may perceive you as communicating critically (Critical Parent) or manipulative (Rebellious Child), wanting something from them. You'll know you've done this if the reciprocal response back is ineffective. If you know that someone is suspicious of Free Child Strokes, don't use them.

10.10 Using positive Strokes to give developmental feedback

Negative Strokes given from an effective ego state are more likely to be heard and provide people with a base from which they can develop, learn, and grow. The most powerful way of providing an effective negative developmental Stroke is by using all three of the effective ego states in balance.

Examples of Strokes from the three effective ego states could be:

Nurturing Parent Strokes:

- How are you? Shows interest in someone
- Creating a welcoming space, bringing the person's preferred drink
- Listening even when you are busy demonstrates to someone that they are important to you
- Giving someone time to work through a problem
- Acknowledging how someone is

Free Child Strokes:

- Being honest about the positive impact someone has had on you, for example, communicating how you were pleased about how they were in a meeting or that they are working well with you
- Swapping ideas, especially where you are enthused by someone else's idea
- Explaining to someone what's been going on for you – demonstrates that you trust them

Adult Strokes:

- Attending to the data together
- Understanding the data or a report they have provided
- Giving additional information
- Helping to solve a problem
- Explaining the rationale for a new expectation or a change
- Repeating information that has already been given

The last four Adult examples on the list above are what we often want to impart as developmental negative Strokes, those improvers. It is through beginning with Nurturing Parent and Free Child positive Strokes that enables an interaction to move more swiftly to a helpful, reciprocal Adult conversation, one that sets a new expectation or points out that there's a different way to do something. By using this method, threat states are thought to be minimised, keeping the PFC open for deep thinking and problem solution. This is a good example of how to use all three effective ego states in balance, as described in Chapters 8 and 9.

10.11 Authentic Strokes

This is particularly difficult if you have a low positive Stroke need and you want to meet the high positive Stroke needs of your colleague, doing your best to use the Platinum rule, there is a good chance that you may try too hard to be giving Strokes that don't sit right with you. You may be using language that is unfamiliar to you or asking your face to smile when you are uncomfortable giving a lot of praise. How do you do all of this if it doesn't feel right? In short don't! If you come across as inauthentic, just saying what you think someone wants to hear you run the risk as coming across as manipulative (Rebellious Child) or being submissive (Compliant Child), neither is likely to have the desired impact.

This is about finding the words that work for you, the parts of the needed Stroke that you can do, finding your own way to meet their needs. For example: if you are uncomfortable with expressing praise you can use phrases such as 'pleased with' or 'I recognise your efforts'. If you have a different Stroke balance to another you can explain why you find it hard to meet their needs as that is not your way and together agree on some ways that you can demonstrate you are doing a bit more of what each other needs: just having that conversation is in itself a positive Stroke. And, you can refer back to Figure 10.1 making sure that you are using more everyday positive Strokes to keep the positive Stroke economy high for someone who needs it.

10.12 Self-refection

- How many and what type of Strokes do you like to receive, especially when you have got something wrong?
- Which ones make you uncomfortable?
- Which and how many do you like to give?
- Do you operate to the golden rule or the platinum rule?
- Is there someone who you work with where you think you may be giving them the wrong type of Strokes? Which Strokes could you give instead?
- Are your negative Strokes coming across as Critical Parent? Can you use more of other effective ego states to deliver recognition? Could you use

either the Free Child or the Nurturing Parent opening to help you to get to an Adult conversation?

- How can you ensure your positive Strokes are authentic? Think about your language and what you are comfortable doing and saying. Perhaps explain to someone else why this is hard. That conversation is itself a positive Stroke

References

Berne, E. (1962). Classification of positions. *Transactional Analysis Bulletin, 1*(3), 23.
Berne, E. (1977). *Games people play: The psychology of human relationships*. Grove Press.
Harris, T. (1969). *I'm OK – you're OK: A practical guide to transactional analysis*. Galahad Books.

Section IV

USING THE TRANSITION TASKS

This section directly applies the transition curve and the psychological tasks of transition introduced in base model 3 in Chapter 3. Throughout this application I use the model to help you understand how to create organisational change, still taking people with you (Chapter 11), and how to influence people (Chapter 12).

DOI:10.4324/9781003623250-14

11

I'M ABOUT TO CREATE CHANGE – HOW DO I DO THAT AND STILL TAKE PEOPLE WITH ME?

How to harness the positivity of a transition: setting and maintaining the environment for change

This chapter differs from most other chapters in this book, as I introduce structural and organisational models of change and pair these with the psychological model of transition. While it's really helpful to understand how humans react when you ask them to change, and to have some psychological insights into how to minimise their resistance, it's also very important to understand the context within which change happens and how to be ready and organise for change, then to keep the momentum of change going. In this chapter, I introduce John Kotter's eight stages of change, which I think is one of the best structural approaches to creating and maintaining change.

We now live in an era of unprecedented change: the consultancy SMRS recently demonstrated that we now experience ten times more change than in 1970, that instead of leading a world towards stability and scale we now have a world that is constantly adapting and changing (Nichols, 2024). Knowing how to harness colleagues' engagement and interest is crucial in this ever-changing world.

In Chapter 3, I introduced the transition curve and the transition tasks, four psychological actions that are vital for engaging people in something new.

The informational tasks:

- Communicating purpose
- Communicating clear direction and expectations

DOI:10.4324/9781003623250-15

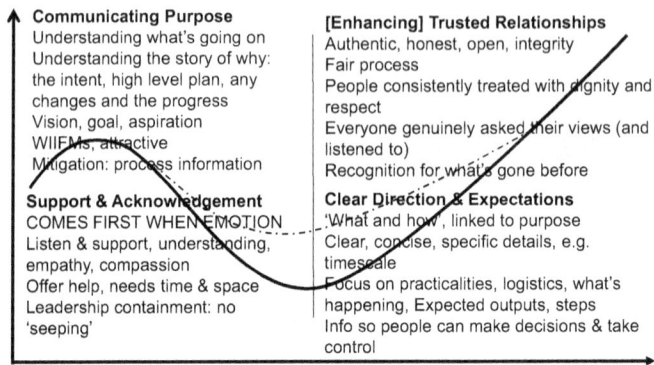

Communicating Purpose
Understanding what's going on
Understanding the story of why:
the intent, high level plan, any
changes and the progress
Vision, goal, aspiration
WIIFMs, attractive
Mitigation: process information

[Enhancing] Trusted Relationships
Authentic, honest, open, integrity
Fair process
People consistently treated with dignity and
respect
Everyone genuinely asked their views (and
listened to)
Recognition for what's gone before

Support & Acknowledgement
COMES FIRST WHEN EMOTION
Listen & support, understanding,
empathy, compassion
Offer help, needs time & space
Leadership containment: no
'seeping'

Clear Direction & Expectations
'What and how', linked to purpose
Clear, concise, specific details, e.g.
timescale
Focus on practicalities, logistics, what's
happening, Expected outputs, steps
Info so people can make decisions & take
control

Figure 11.1 The tasks of transition that help us to adapt to change

The relational tasks:

•   Supporting and acknowledging
•   Enhancing trusted relationships

Transition is the internal process of adapting to change – it's what a human goes through as we process and adjust to a change. While it is a very important model, it's most helpful for considering how to support and individual through change. When contemplating systemic change there's a well-known structure that this internal process is only a part of. In this chapter, I look at how to set the environment for systemic change: it's particularly helpful for setting up a new project team, when there's a restructure or for introducing a new process or concept. If you are unsure where to focus your energy when creating change, my advice is to use the structural approach described here for whole system change and refer back to the transition curve when focusing on individuals (also see Chapter 12 on using the transition curve to influence).

The structural approaches I like best come from the work of Kurt Lewin (1951), considered one of the founders of organisational change theory, and John Kotter's (1996) eight steps model of change management. When Googled, these rank highly in the most searched change models. Both look at stages of change and what's needed to start change or a project off strongly, what's necessary to sustain and maintain the change, and what helps them to finish strongly, so that the next change can have focus. Today, as we encounter multiple changes at once, we may have to carry out actions from each stage.

Lewin was a physicist turned psychologist: his analogy was that you need to unfreeze attitudes in order to change, then mould a new way of thinking. This means empowering people to change and finally refreeze

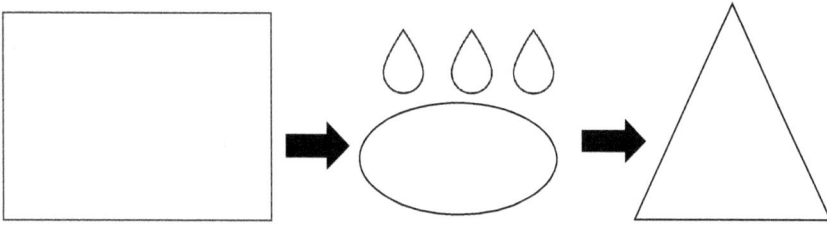

Figure 11.2 Unfreeze, change, refreeze (Lewin, 1951)

the attitude as new ways of thinking so that you create a new stability. John Kotter kept these three phases, growing what's needed into eight stages overall.

11.1 Kotter's three phases and eight stages of change

Table 11.1 Kotter's phases and stages of change

Phase 1	Stage 1	Establish a sense of urgency
Create climate for change	Stage 2	Create the guiding coalition
	Stage 3	Develop a change vision
Phase 2	Stage 4	Communicate the vision for buy-in
Engage and enable the whole	Stage 5	Empower broad-based action
organisation	Stage 6	Generate short-term wins
Phase 3	Stage 7	Never let up
Implement and sustain change	Stage 8	Incorporate change into culture

11.1.1 Phase 1: Create the climate for change: urgency, the guiding coalition and vision

What happens at the beginning of a change process is considered the most important phase of change. Most energy is needed in these early three stages where you create the climate for change: hard work, careful planning and building these foundations for change are essential to increase the chances that it will work.

Stage 1: establish urgency by determining need – seeing what can be better. Key tasks here are to explain why the change is needed, what the benefits will be, thus engaging people in conversation by starting a dialogue, developing the case for change and possibly a problem-solving process. This is about getting ready and creates momentum. From a personal transition perspective, this is about how a human engages in a change process: this activity represents the 'purpose task' – as no human will change unless there's a good reason for it.

99

Stage 2: the guiding coalition. One of the key structural conditions needed is a 'guiding coalition': this is the name given to the first person or people involved. This is a group convened for the purpose of this initiative, members of which are generally in agreement and by the time the change begins, on the same page. They spearhead the change, even if what they are bringing is unpopular. Through their actions, they help others to similarly recognise the need for change. They create the sense of momentum and urgency which provides the energy for change and dissonance against it. In this model, dissonance is expected and not to be fought against or coerced, as Kotter noted that resistance worsens if people are cajoled or coerced.

This is often described as getting ready to go into battle. The guiding coalition needs to include people who can really influence change. Kotter's model reflects a belief of the time (in 1996) in the power of the hierarchy; these people would be expected to take ownership, reflecting that most, but not all, organisational change needs to be modelled and supported from the top. Today, we'd expect that this coalition is more diverse, with participation from a range of perspectives. For example, collaborating with middle managers as strategic partners in these decisions and activities creates an enabling bridge between top and bottom. However, in my experience, having senior management endorsement makes it work better.

The sense of urgency and energy needs to be maintained and is characterised by enthusiastic meetings. An important realisation of Kotter's model is that the more people get involved, the more likely that the initial idea may change. This is hard for the 'inventor or creator' who often wants to hold on to their idea of change. I've often thought this is a useful concept to remember: Kotter describes change as 'a snowball rolling down a hill', meaning that its shape evolves. If the initial advocate insists the change stays in the same form, this attitude is considered a point of potential failure for a change project.

Stage 3: developing the vision. Whatever is happening is now more than an idea, it's now a strategic objective and becomes built into the fabric of the vision, which can now be worked up into something more concrete and compelling – there's now a formal description of something people can buy into. This needs to be expressed in a way that is easy to understand: this is an important psychological facet, part of the Clear Direction Task, as too much information overwhelms the tired brain – and tired brains are what we encounter when multiple changes are occurring. Overall, in this phase, you're engaging about the vision not the detail.

In new project teams, this phase is the most crucial: sometimes the vision is not the correct one to work on, in which case the starting point is checking that the team is engaged on the 'right thing'. Years and resources have been wasted on setting up project teams to do the 'wrong thing'. Agreeing who the guiding coalition will be is important: this depends as much on who has time as who has enthusiasm. Determining the urgency depends on setting the project rhythm or cadence right from the start; this means working out how the team comes together and when, including setting their norms, language and agreeing simple things like the digital tools to be used.

11.1.2 Phase 2: Engage and enable the whole system (or organisation): communicate vision, empower and demonstrate early wins

These three stages are all about making the change actually happen; this phase is less energetic, more considered, there are more plans and details needed to enable and engage.

Stage 4: communication. Now every possible communication vehicle is used. This is as much about effective communication skills as role modelling the change, where the guiding coalition needs to be demonstrating how the change will work, leading the way. They are out there talking enthusiastically about the changes, engaging with people, so creating an effective cascade. This is another key point where change projects fail.

Numerous studies of change projects over the years have demonstrated that the main reason they fail is because resistance isn't addressed. Understanding the process of transition by referring to the transition curve (Chapter 3) helps to identify what is happening and minimise resistance.

Kotter was the first person to overtly address resistance and the need for psychological safety as a key requirement needed to reduce resistance. Transition curves became popular in organisations around this time to help people through the emotions underlying resistance, usually anger, anxiety and loss. These curves were developed from the psychiatrist Elizabeth Kubler-Ross's work on bereavement (1969): now every leadership development consultant has a version of the transition curve to help to explain the process humans go

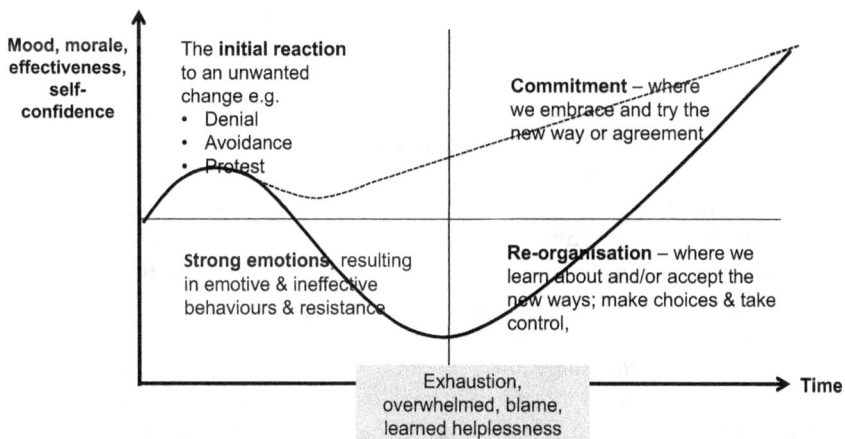

Figure 11.3 The transition curve showing how humans adjust to change

101

through when confronted with unwanted or challenging change. The transition curve I use then goes on to look at the four tasks, essentially the four types of communication, needed to ensure optimal adjustment to change (see Figure 11.1).

Holding regular psychological safety activities help, where colleagues can share their feelings about the proposed ideas and the impact this will have on them. These listening activities have an important role to play in minimising resistance and increasing engagement. For example, in dedicated project teams, such activities provide an opportunity to revise and check levels of commitment, as it's common to find that, since the advent of the project, key members of the guiding coalition have been pulled elsewhere.

Stage 5: the empower step is all about removing barriers, including resistance, which is why it needs addressing. Other common barriers to change are structures, systems, processes and, most of all, time. Here, the obstacles are explored, understood and, where possible, removed. These need to be identified as the process unfolds and may include moving people or changing processes or priorities to free up time. Regular conversations about blockers and how to solve them is another useful forum in this phase. Another empowerment activity is to check that those with responsibility for a particular element of the programme are able to keep to their objectives, to keep 'in their swim lane'. If they aren't, some understanding of what's happening is needed to see whether other resources or structures could better serve the overall objective.

Stage 6: creating short term wins is thought to be a good vehicle for keeping people motivated or tipping more people into engagement, as these show the change is worthwhile and is fulfilling the vision and purpose set at the beginning. These need to be highly visible. It is also important to recognise those involved for their efforts, so that they maintain their energy.

11.1.3 Phase 3: Implement and sustain change: never let up and incorporate into culture

Stage 7: never let up. In order to implement and sustain change, there needs to be demonstration of a series of consolidated improvements, where successes or small wins are built on. If there's a setback, you aim to showcase a different small win. Showing the data is important – people like proof; if you've measured throughout, you will have data to demonstrate it's working. According to Kotter, another way to consolidate improvement is to bring new energy in, so you now recruit or promote people who can implement the vision, who will steer it and keep it going.

Stage 8: incorporate change into the culture. Eventually, a change becomes business as usual: it's important to have closure by recognising the new ways of working are successful, demonstrating that change worked and was worthwhile as well as building the new ways into training and cultural expectations.

Retrospective activities that include all these involved, such as lessons learnt or celebrations of success, tend to be overlooked in busy organisations. These provide the needed confidence boosts, where we recognise how much we've learnt and been able to do, as well as provide recognition and validation. These activities make available the neurotransmitter substances that provide satisfaction and joy. Without these final experiences people remember the difficulties they encountered, not the satisfaction of making something new happen.

11.2 Self-reflection

Check your change programme or project for the following features that go wrong and congratulate yourself when you've got these in place:

- How have you established urgency? Do you have a good purpose and a compelling vision? Is this articulated simply?
- How well does your guiding coalition work? Are you aligned? Do you have the right people? Do you have the influence to make change happen? Have you reviewed who does what and when? Do roles or priorities need to change?
- If this change is your 'baby', are you clinging on too hard to your original idea?
- Are you curious about resistance to the change? Do you understand why people are cautious (or worse)?
- Are you struggling to support an individual through a change process? Are you encountering a resistant colleague? Go back to Chapter 3 and consider the transition tasks in more detail
- Have you been looking for and exploring barriers? Do you have problem solution sessions for these?
- Have roles in steering the change become confused or conflicted? If so have you reassessed who does what and when?
- Have you been communicating short term wins?
- Did you celebrate the end of your last change initiative?

References

Kotter, J.P. (1996). *Leading Change.* Harvard Business School Press

Kübler-Ross, E. (1969). *On death and dying: What the dying have to teach doctors, nurses, clergy and their own families.* Macmillan.

Lewin, K. (1951). *Field Theory in Social Science.* Harper.

Nichols, S. (2024, 30 July). *The future of leadership development* [Webinar]. SMRS. https://www.eventbrite.co.uk/e/webinar-future-of-leadership-development-tickets-916111262447

12

HOW DO I INFLUENCE WHEN SOMEONE IS RESISTANT AND DEFENSIVE?

The psychology of influencing

The psychological tasks of transition is my go-to model when working with leaders to influence effectively. I start by making the case that all leadership is influencing, then move on to who we can influence and the amount of power and influence we actually have. Then I take the four psychological tasks of transition one by one, demonstrating how to use each to be influential. You'll need all four in place to be an effective influencer. To understand how to influence effectively you will need to have read all three base models to get the best from this chapter.

Influencing is all about getting someone else to follow: we are really looking at the 'art of followership', how to get someone else to become engaged in your message especially when it is something that doesn't interest them or when they have a different viewpoint.

When I map the impact of a successful influencer on the transition curve, I note that they use all four transition tasks, delivered using the effective, blue ego states. This chapter pulls out in more detail what needs to be communicated in each task, specifically to influence someone who is sceptical or resistant.

12.1 Who can we influence?

First, it's important to consider who we can influence. This definition from the business school Roffey Park's training programme sums it up for me 'influencing is everything we say or don't say, do or don't do, that modifies, affects, or changes someone else's behaviour, thoughts, or actions, consciously or unconsciously' (McBrown, n.d). Our very presence at a meeting may influence people positively or negatively. The style or nature of our presence, what we say or how we say it and the attitude we project speaks volumes. I am also clear about what influencing is not: one dictionary defines influencing as 'the power or sway resulting from ability, wealth or position'. However, I believe that effective workplace influencing is not about exerting

DOI:10.4324/9781003623250-16

power or beating people into submission, it's a process that engages people, not causes them to be brow-beaten.

Dilbert author, Scott Adams, is widely quoted to have said 'you don't have to be a person of influence to be influential'. Whatever our hierarchical position is, we all have influence: according to my colleague Sarah Brooks (2024) we have power that I think translates into influence:

1. Referent influence: the ability to convince more senior others of your argument
2. Expert influence: being recognised as knowing more about a subject
3. Informational influence: having more or different information to support your arguments

When we hold leadership positions we also have:

4. 'Legitimate' influence: the authority to issue instructions with the expectation that these will be carried through
5. Reward influence: which is access to valued rewards that will be distributed in return for engagement

Using Stephen Covey's Circle, or Sphere, of Influence (1989) also helps us to think about who we can influence. His diagram of three concentric circles demonstrates the three sets of people whom we can influence:

1. Ourselves, as we have direct control over how we think, behave and act
2. Those people whom we can directly influence: we are most effective influencers when we influence those we actually have access to
3. Those whom we have concerns about, where we don't have direct influencing ability. Much time is wasted at work trying to influence someone about something we're concerned about, where we don't have access to them. I've seen too many people waste their resources trying to directly influence someone they don't know and don't have sufficient referent influence, instead of working out an effective influence strategy. In this situation we are better using our energy to influence through someone else

We know when we are being successful. If we are engaging someone or seeing resistance there are characteristic responses. When someone is engaged in our message they'll show interest, maybe be absorbed, they'll make an emotional connection, saying something that mirrors your and their experiences. They'll show some form of connection to what you've said and are likely to carry through with what you are asking.

If they are resistant, they'll respond in Rebellious or Compliant Child, they are likely to show some form of threat response: they may avoid, complain or be slow to respond. They won't become involved and will be slow to change. It's this resistance that the four tasks of transition help us with as long as we deliver these using the three effective ego states.

12.2 Using the four tasks of transition to influence

In this section, I will build on what I've already outlined about how to use the four tasks of transition.

12.2.1 Communicating purpose

In summary, here we give good quality, high level information where we explain why we want something doing, why something is happening. We match this to someone's needs (also see reward and threat prompts in Chapter 5) and style. In particular, when influencing, there are some key methods of communicating purpose.

According to David Clutterbuck (2023), team members need to hear three types of purpose communications:

1. Pragmatic purpose: describing short term objectives and why
2. Grounded purpose: the desired impact on the local landscape and immediate stakeholders
3. Higher purpose: communicates the overarching impact, perhaps on the end user or the wider societal impact

However, if those purpose statements are not meaningful to an individual, they are less likely to follow. When an individual has a good purpose for something, particularly a values-aligned purpose, there's good evidence that this improves neurological functioning and thereby performance. It is one of

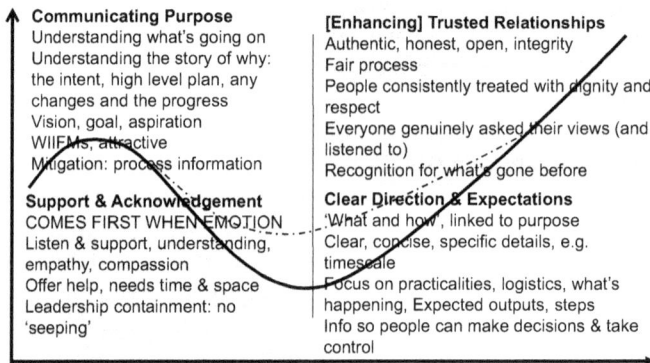

Figure 12.1 The four tasks of transition

the only mechanisms where the PFC can override high limbic system stimulation. So, it's important for us to be working on something that has personal purpose for the other too. The starting point here is to at least understand the other's purpose in this situation. Knowing what's motivating them and matching your message to that insight is important: when we don't, suspicion, doubt and misunderstanding creep in.

Practical steps to take here include considering how compelling your narrative is. There are a number of elements to constructing a compelling purpose, including how attractive it is to another, how the message is framed, or explained, and the construction of the 'story'.

12.2.1.1 Attractiveness

How do we make an unattractive message engaging? We turn it round and emphasise the good bits, the elements of the issue that will help. Many of us will have bought all sorts of things over the years based on attractiveness even though when we get the item home it's not that attractive at all. Advertising is built on this principle.

In day-to-day work-based influencing, where we want to remain ethical, this is not about kidding people, it is about finding the positives. As we've noted from the neuroscience underpinning leadership, if the message is negative, our limbic systems fire quickly, a threat has been created and our brains will become defensive. An element of attractiveness needs to be found to prevent this, to create a reward state, and it needs to be an ethical one.

For example, an organisation I worked in a while ago changed their reward structure. Overall, this is what the workforce had been requesting for a while; however, in the short term, those performing well would miss out on a small bonus in the first year. This was announced with a great deal of trepidation although highlighting the opportunities and why they were doing it, demonstrating senior leaders had listened and stressing the other long-term benefits meant that their influencing worked well.

12.2.1.2 Framing

If I tell you a story, however interesting, but I don't explain why I'm engaging you in the first place, then you are far less likely to listen. I need to tell you why I'm telling you that story in order to engage you in the story to start with. This is 'framing', sometimes called signposting.

Consider these contrasting starts to a meeting:

(a) 'Good morning, I hope that I'm not going to bore you today as there are loads of facts and figures we need to go through'

OR

(b) 'Good morning, I've a lot of really important information that I want to bring to your attention today. We'd better get started'

Which is most appealing? The second gives a reason to engage even with a difficult subject while the first is more likely to be greeted with resistance and groans.

Framing has a powerful impact on what we focus on and how we invite someone to engage, particularly if we talk from our own perspective or experience, using the words 'I' or 'me', thereby communicating with the Free Child ego state. This is because of the reciprocal impact this is likely to have, offering another to respond from interest, Nurturing Parent, or to engage on an emotional level. This 'emotional hook' is considered very important in creating followership.

A good frame, a good reason, gives us purpose and an initial reason to follow. A frame or signpost informing us about what's going to happen and how takes away some of our uncertainty or anxiety and helps us to be more in control – all reward mechanisms. This is why teachers and lecturers are encouraged to use sections of lessons setting out what is about to happen. We need to 're-frame' to attract different audiences: one frame doesn't work for all. For example, some groups prefer data-driven or highly fact-based frames compared to others who prefer to hear about the social value or personal reasons. Assessing what will be attractive to different audiences then tailoring the frame is key when influencing.

12.2.1.3 Constructing a compelling story

People follow stories: we relate to, and enjoy, the suspense of an unfolding narrative. It gives us an explanation for what is happening and, if well told, establishes the point. Stories are thought to be heard more easily especially when there is threat and resistance. There's good research to suggest that story telling produces more oxytocin, one of the substances we need to calm the limbic system, than other forms of communication (Zak, 2014).

When stories are broken down, they usually consist of the following elements:

1. The story of me – why I got involved, why this matters to me, why this is urgent, important, special for me. These insights into another person give the story credibility. The absence of this personal story is often what decreases a narrative's credibility and limits emotional buy-in. This is a highly Free Child, authentic communication
2. The story of us – this part of the story explains why something is valuable to you both. It may remind us of our shared history, our common purpose, the higher vision. This is often the reasoning in the story, the 'facts' the more logical section, the Adult communication

3.   The story of now – this tells a powerful narrative about why we need to do this together, the benefits this will have for us all and what we'll share as a result. This part of a narrative binds us together. This is the Nurturing Parent narrative. A common mistake at this point of the story is to tell someone the benefits there will be to 'me' not the common benefits for 'us'

An effective story will mirror the language and culture of the audience: for example, a story that mirrors scientific method is more likely to appeal to a scientific community than one focused on supposition and intangibles.

12.2.2 Communicating clear direction and expectations

Once the purpose has been grasped and colleagues have a reason to engage in doing something different, it's now time to focus on what it is you want or need them to do. The essence of this psychological task is clarity. This means having a concise, easy to understand message about what is expected and how and when it is to be achieved. This is the explanation of the details, the next steps, the criteria for success and any consequences for poor performance.

There are some simple guidelines for delivering such messages:

*   This is where you use facts and information. This is the task that requires really clear Adult ego state communication: factual, logical, without judgement or emotion
*   Focus on what and how: the practicalities, logistics, what's happening, expected outputs, steps, and how to remove obstacles
*   Clear, concise expression of what you want: remember the overloaded brain gets muddled when there's too much information. To prevent overload, use 'layers': communicate a piece of the message, once that's understood, layer on a little more
*   Be realistic and fair, especially if these are threat prompts to your colleagues. Tailor the message so that it meets the reward needs of your team: for example, if you have people with validation and / or control reward needs, make sure you include demonstrations of these in your narrative
*   Prepare to compromise or work together on new emergent ideas: often when we get to this point someone else has a brilliant idea that may eclipse our planned expectation. Ignoring this risks disengagement and a Compliant Child response to your request
*   If you are in disagreement or challenged, know your bottom line. Negotiation theory teaches us that being clear about what we will and won't compromise on, and why, knowing what alternatives we'll accept and what we can 'trade', all help both parties engagement in an effective outcome

All of this requires preparation, some prior thought about what you want to say, how you'll say it, how it's likely to be received and how you may need to alter the narrative for different groups or individuals to meet their particular needs. Key guidance when addressing teams is to speak to the biggest group: for example, if you have more people with success and achievement reward needs, emphasise that message, then go back and address those with differing needs afterwards.

12.2.3 Using the support and acknowledgement task to influence

Every book or study I've ever read tells me that this is the most important task when influencing. Are you surprised, as there's no imparting of any facts here, so how can this be influential?

Attunement, the understanding of someone else's needs and motivations is considered fundamental to successful influencing and negotiation. How well you know what the other person is wanting to get from a situation and how much they are prepared to psychologically invest has a direct impact on the outcome. Do you understand their reticence or defensiveness?

Extensive research from the Programme on Negotiation at Harvard Law School (https://www.pon.harvard.edu/) has shown that effective influencers probe their counterparts to better understand their underlying interests. They understand someone's point of view, where they are coming from and why, they show empathy, demonstrating a preparedness to listen and understand. This starts with curiosity and listening, thereby beginning the process of focusing on them as people with needs, not a game to win or a set of ideas or actions to impose (see Figure 12.2). The opposite of this is to assume what they are thinking, needing or intending: the act of assuming can easily

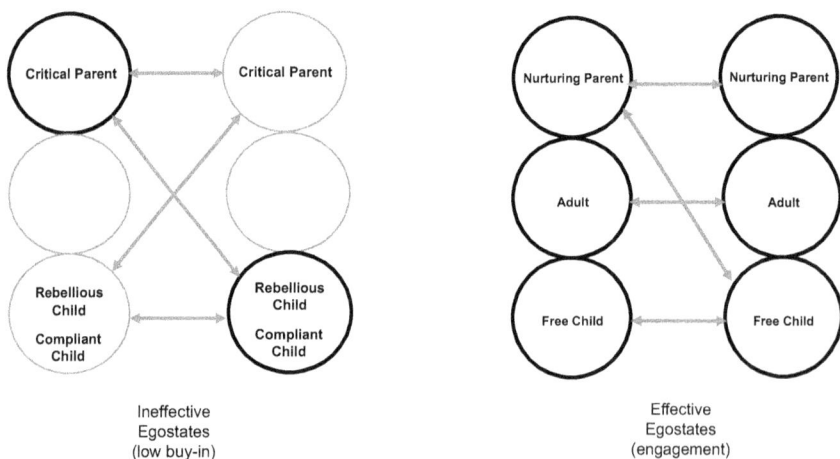

Ineffective
Egostates
(low buy-in)

Effective
Egostates
(engagement)

Figure 12.2 The ego state: reciprocal transactions

be seen as a threatening behaviour, perhaps as Critical Parent or Rebellious Child and so would be met reciprocally by a threatened, defensive or judgemental response.

The same researchers, Fisher and Ury, in their book on negotiation, *Getting to Yes* (2012), demonstrated that effective negotiators listen four times more than they speak. By doing this you help someone be psychologically ready for the facts and expectations that you want (and have prepared) to put across.

Sarah Brooks, a researcher on 'Voice', the sharing of upward communication, highlighted that 85% of people at work withhold voice at some point at work (Brooks, 2024; Milliken et al., 2003). They don't speak up due to fear, especially with their managers. This brings into sharp focus the importance of hearing that voice, those concerns. Such research demonstrates that not listening has a detrimental impact on organisational effectiveness. In other words, not listening, hearing and understanding means what you are trying to influence has much less chance of working (for more on voice, see Chapter 15).

Fundamentally listening and understanding to how people feel is a crucial task of managing someone's personal transition, even when you fundamentally disagree with their response. Giving someone an emotional outlet is often the step needed to help them to think about and process what it is you are wanting from them. It is now well established that when someone is experiencing a strong emotion one of the most effective actions they can take is to name the emotion. Supporting them to express what's going on for them and why, especially talking about their concerns, means the limbic system is temporarily less stimulated, allowing the PFC to dominate so that they can think more logically.

Actions in this task aren't just about responding considerately to others' emotional responses, it is also about managing our own. A key activity here is becoming aware of and acknowledging one's own reactions, then taking steps to manage these through resilience techniques (as described in Chapter 4). Showing your own frustration to another's response of defensiveness or resistance will only make the other more resistant and disengaged, moving you both towards a conflict loop.

12.2.4 The importance of the enhancing trusted relationships task in influencing

I've often wondered why this task comes last in the depiction of the four transition tasks as it's the one we need to be present all the way through. People are far more likely to follow us, our message and our expectations if there is a good relationship and trust between us. Investing in a relationship before you need to influence them to do something they may not want to is going to make it easier. However, all is not lost: behaving transparently, with integrity, showing voluntary vulnerability and being a real person are likely to make a difference and go a long way to creating the psychological safety that's needed here.

Once again it's key to match your relationship building techniques to the needs of the other, being highly open and honest about what's going on for you. Free Child won't work well with someone who is a big Adult, so mirror the other's needs and style. Use that 'platinum rule' (see Chapter 10).

The golden and platinum rules of getting the best from people

Golden Rule: treat people how you'd like to be treated
Platinum Rule: treat people how they'd like to be treated

What's needed here is oxytocin, that neurotransmitter substance secreted when there is a good bond between us that decreases threat states. Using behavioural stakeholder mapping tools, (for example, the one used in Chapter 15) can help us to decide what the other person needs from us in order to trust.

Another way of approaching this task is to think about what makes you an effective influencer or leader and, using the skills that you particularly believe in, fulfilling what I call your 'leadership philosophy'; this will mean you are behaving with integrity and being true to yourself.

A set of key behavioural indicators that increase trust, when influencing and negotiating include:

- Being grateful and recognising other's contributions, especially if they are going out of their way to do something that is hard for them or that they don't want to do
- Maintaining respect, in particular being prepared to listen and understand, not dismiss, concerns
- Being prepared to co-create another solution, so not sticking rigidly to your desired outcome. There are often other good ideas

12.3 Influencing: the order matters

Influencing using the four tasks of transition works best using a formula:

1. When there's good relationship and little resistance, Purpose and Clear Direction are likely to work on their own, although don't neglect the two relational tasks
2. When there's little engagement or followership, any defensiveness or resistance, then start with two relational tasks, 'Support' and

'Acknowledgement', and work on enhancing the relationship in tandem with the informational tasks

12.4 Self-reflection

- Are you influencing the right person? Is this someone you can actually influence?
- Have you been using elements of all these four tasks when influencing?
- More specifically, think about some key elements of effective influencing; how do you think you are doing in general?
    - Do you consider how attractive your purpose is to someone else? Could you reframe it?
    - Framing – do you explain why something is happening?
    - Do you tell a story or is your narrative a set of demands?
    - How clear are your expectations? Are you overwhelming people with information?
    - Are you flexible? If so, do you think about your bottom line?
    - Do you prepare before you influence?
    - How much do you invest in understanding the other's perspective, needs and reactions?
    - How much do you listen?
    - How well do you manage your own frustration when influencing?
    - How much do you invest in a trusted relationship with those you want to influence?
- Think of someone you want to influence more effectively: which task and what activities in that task could help you if you did this more?

References

Brooks, S. (2024). Coaching as a Route to Voice: A Framework for Change. *The Coaching Psychologist, 20*(1), 50–62. https://doi.org/10.53841/bpstcp.2024.20.1.50

Clutterbuck, D. (2023). Three levels of purpose. *Clutterbuck Coaching and Mentoring International.* https://clutterbuck-cmi.com/blogs/three-levels-of-purpose/

Covey, S.R. (1989). *The 7 habits of highly effective people.* Simon & Schuster.

Fisher, R., & Ury, W. (2012) *Getting to yes: Negotiating an agreement without giving in.* Random House Business.

McBrown, J. (n.d.). *What is influence and what are influencing skills?* Roffey Park Institute. https://www.roffeypark.com/articles/what-is-influence-and-what-are-influencing-skills/

Milliken, F.J., Morrison, E.W., & Hewlin, P.F. (2003). An exploratory study of employee silence: Issues that employees don't communicate upward and why. *Journal of Management Studies, 40*(6), 1453–1476.

Zak, P.J. (2014, 28 October). Why your brain loves good storytelling. *Harvard Business Review.* https://hbr.org/2014/10/why-your-brain-loves-good-storytelling

Section V

USING ALL THREE MODELS
IN COMBINATION

This section tackles the hardest leadership activities, such as giving feedback so that it is acted upon, instilling ownership, how to be heard and leading a whole team. All three of the base models, used in combination, are needed to approach these.

DOI:10.4324/9781003623250-17

13

HOW DO I GIVE CHALLENGING FEEDBACK SO ITS HEARD AND ACTED UPON?

The art of feedback: 'the most threat inducing act of leadership'

One of the leadership gurus that I follow considers the giving and receiving of challenging, or even constructive, feedback to be one of the most difficult activities of leadership. I certainly think it's something that frequently doesn't work very well or is often avoided. This chapter considers the relevance and use of all three base models: effective feedback needs to be delivered from the effective ego states in order to minimise threat states. Feedback given and received in reward states will be better acted upon – I look at how to get there. Since developmental feedback is asking someone to do something different the transition curve, explaining why we resist, and the transition tasks that show us what we need in place to be engaged with, give us a neat sequence for giving feedback. Becoming more and more practical as the chapter progresses, I also look at specific feedback techniques from TA (make sure you've read Chapter 10 on the Strokes), recent neuroscience (see Chapter 5 on threat and reward prompts) and specific research into effective feedback.

13.1 Effective feedback

Whenever I deliver this topic in leadership development forums, I ask groups to tell me what makes their developmental or challenging feedback work. They always bring a comprehensive list which I organise as shown in Table 13.1 into a demonstration of the three effective ego states.

I arrange it this way as a very simple truth of giving any form of feedback is that it works best when delivered using all three of the effective ego states. In particular where there's emotion, usually manifesting as frustration and defensiveness on both sides, the Nurturing Parent and Free Child communications are what makes the necessary Adult message heard. Starting and staying in Adult risks perception of Critical Parent, with Compliant and Rebellious Child responses and edges us towards a conflict loop (see

DOI: 10.4324/9781003623250-18

Table 13.1 The effective ego states and effective feedback

Nurturing Parent	Adult	Free Child
• Set up the space to support confidential conversations • Ask for their viewpoint before you give yours • Take a coaching approach • Curious questions • Listening and ask supplementary questions • Be prepared to understand what lies beneath • Show empathy, demonstrate that you know this is hard • Supporting the success of the other	• Frame the conversation, say why you're there • Outline the process for the conversation • Ask questions for data or clarification and listen to responses • Deliver feedback succinctly • Be specific, use actual examples and data • Describe the consequences (if something is not being done) • Be clear about the expectation • Stay firm by repeating the expectation • All of this prepared in advance	• Be honest • Talk about yourself and the impact on you • Describe why this conversation/situation is important to you • Explain why you need something doing a particular way • Manage own emotions • Be prepared to be flexible and work with new ideas

Chapter 10 for a description of how to use positive Strokes and all three effective ego states to give developmental feedback). In other words, feedback is heard and acted upon best when we manage to reduce the threat.

13.2 The impact of feedback

Researchers at the Neuroleadership Institute demonstrated that both the receiving and giving of unsolicited feedback was highly anxiety inducing, demonstrated by erratic heart rates. Even saying that you're about to receive some feedback elicited similar results. Tessa West and Katherine Thorson (2018), at New York University, showed that difficult feedback was the activity leaders most dreaded, and direct reports were most wary about. Their research highlighted the amount of threat often inherent in feedback conversations. The threat of giving challenging feedback can mean the PFC is not well accessed, therefore, the feedback is often not well planned or articulated and during the conversation thought errors, biases or commonly overplayed strengths are more likely to manifest.

Similarly, in the moment of receiving feedback someone disagrees with or finds hard, it is likely to elicit a threat state: the feedback may not be properly heard or processed, meaning that responses are more likely to be driven by the limbic system than the PFC, explaining why leaders have the experience of knowing they told someone but not understanding why the response is defensive or even not heard.

There are, of course, many people who thrive on challenging feedback, who see it as a gift and a learning opportunity. If you are a leader who is like this, remember that a significant proportion of those you lead will be having a very different experience to you and you will need to adapt your feedback giving for them.

13.3 The art of feedback: what works?

Feedback is a topic much written about and it troubles me that one high level method for delivering it that has been firmly and psychologically disproved is still suggested. Have you heard of the 'shit sandwich'? This is where you offer positive feedback, or a positive Stroke, followed by the 'meat', the 'what is wrong' and what you want to be different, and then end with something positive again. This does not prevent threat: the anticipation of hearing what is often a bland positive message signals something bad is coming. Worse, hearing positive–negative–positive enacts the 'primacy and recency' effect where we hear and remember the first and last things that are said to us in difficult situations. These being positive, you are thereby unlikely to see any change when using this method.

In Strokes literature, from TA, the accepted method is two positives followed by a single developmental Stroke (as a reminder, a Stroke is a unit of recognition: see Chapter 10 for a full description). There are some caveats: the positives need to be specific examples where someone did something well, followed by a well prepared, succinct and specific improvement or developmental statement. Only when the positive Strokes are authentically delivered and meaningful to the receiver will they reduce threat in order for the expectation statement to be heard.

13.4 Using conditional and unconditional Strokes

As well as positive and negative Strokes, we can also think of Strokes as being conditional, for doing something, or unconditional, for being someone.

- A conditional Stroke is one we receive where it is contingent on something we have done. It's one we give or receive for doing something
- An unconditional Stroke is one we give to someone else simply for being who they are

Using a combination of positive and negative, conditional and positive unconditional Strokes is helpful when giving feedback. Avoid the use of the negative unconditional, these are very damaging and to be avoided. When giving feedback the following are helpful:

- *Positive conditional* Strokes are the most effective way to give people positive feedback. These are specific, so people know exactly what they've done well. Delivering these authentically from Free Child with Adult content makes them more likely to be heard
- *Positive unconditional* Strokes are very powerful in building a strong sense of team spirit and loyalty. They give people the message that they belong, they fit in and that they are valued. Positive unconditional Strokes become ever more important in times of uncertainty, complexity or when times are tough, as long as they meet that person's needs (see below for tailoring feedback to the individual). These are delivered from the Nurturing Parent and Free Child ego states
- *Negative conditional* Strokes are essential in managing poor performance and in giving people developmental feedback. The key thing to bear in mind is to deliver negative conditional Strokes clearly as coming from the effective ego states, otherwise the risk is they will simply be rejected and elicit resentment and the ineffective ego states. These need a clear Adult message, prefaced by using Free Child, why you are giving the feedback, helps them to stick

Consider the examples in Table 13.2.

Table 13.2 Examples of conditional and unconditional Strokes

Positive conditional	Positive unconditional
'That's a good *idea*'	'What a great *team*'
'These *figures* are great'	'I want *you* all to be *involved* in this'
'I appreciate the *time* it's taken to do that'	'I'm glad I'm working *with you* on this project'
A performance related bonus	Being actively listened to
Being asked for expert opinion	Being included in decisions affecting you
Getting extra responsibilities on account of past performance	Being informed of the impact of a change

Negative conditional	Negative unconditional
'The way you treated that customer was not up to scratch *because ...*'	'You're not paid to think, just do it'
'I'm disappointed with this report *because ...*'	'We'll tell you when you need to know'
'This proposal isn't good enough *because...*'	'This team is useless'
Being moved sideways following poor performance	Being excluded from decisions affecting you
Being excluded from tasks because of poor performance	Being over-protected from the impact of change
Failing to gain accreditation because standards were not met	Being criticised in public
	All the 'isms': i.e., racism, sexism, ageism
	Use of the negative unconditional is not recommended

Using the negative unconditional is critical; these are direct judgements about the person. These are Critical Parent communications that have no part in effective feedback. They are damaging, destroy trust and decrease engagement. The Critical Parent impact is sometimes unintended, so work very hard to communicate what you want in a far more helpful way by using all three effective ego states. This type of communication is so damaging we have laws and work policies to restrict some of them – this includes the expression of any bias.

13.5 Reducing threat: tailoring feedback to individual need

In Chapter 5, I introduced threat prompts and reward types. Knowing which reward types a colleague needs really helps so that you can plan your feedback to have an optimal impact for them.

This is all about knowing what to do to avoid creating a threat for them, instead presenting the feedback so that their brain can hear and process your expectations and thinking. Table 13.3 has specific suggestions about what to include and avoid to reduce threat and increase reward depending on someone's threat prompts.

13.6 Using structures for giving feedback

Having a framework for a difficult conversation can be helpful to stay on track and know what to do in the trickiest segments. One has already been suggested, the use of the transition tasks which focus on the behaviours needed to engage someone to do something differently, to influence them. In this section, I also suggest an alternative structure, the GROW model, which is more a way of structuring the conversation.

Using the transition tasks in feedback gives us an order for the feedback:

1. *Start with the purpose:* why are you here, what is this feedback for? This links feedback to the organisational goals, the vision the strategic plan and their objectives. It's also an opportunity for you to state why this meeting is of importance to you. Framing the opportunities for the other is also a useful beginning. When you need to be more circumspect, where for good reasons you cannot be transparent, then also inform about the process, what's going to happen and why

2. *Next be clear about the expectation,* be succinct, layer and get into the practicalities. You are providing information so that people can make decisions and take control

3. *Using the support and acknowledgement task*: if there are any signs of discomfort, defensiveness or disagreement the transition tasks model tells us to go straight to support and acknowledgement where we focus on asking

Table 13.3 Tailoring feedback depending on threat and reward type

Threat prompt/reward type	Specific feedback actions likely to create threat	To build or maintain a reward state when giving feedback
Validation, recognition and affirmation	Ignore contribution Don't recognise experience or skill Take credit for their work Low number of positive Strokes Going straight to the negatives, improver or developmental feedback	Thank for contributions Recognise experience and skill Public acknowledgment of contribution, experience, skill Gratitude for previous effort and for participating in the difficult conversation Will need a higher positive to developmental Strokes ratio
Control, agency and predictability	Being vague about what's happening, why here and what's expected Taking away responsibility Micromanagement Changing something without explanation Overloading the person without clear priorities	Explanation of why things are happening Very clear expectations Clarity about next steps Given clear choices A clear plan for what's next Support with prioritising Create predictability and certainty
Support, acknowledgement and being heard	No opportunity for the other to give their view Poor listening, understanding and empathy Too much 'tell' Judging without understanding	Active listening (four times more than speaking) Ask curious questions Understand, empathise and show compassion Set aside time to do the above Activities that enhance relationships and trust Being prepared to run with their suggestions

Having a good purpose	Fail to explain why:
	  You are here
	  Why this feedback is being given
	  How the feedback links to their objectives
	  How the feedback links to organisational success
	  Only consider your purpose, not theirs too
		Focus more on purpose than you would for another by explaining the three types of purpose:
		1. Higher: overarching organisational purpose
		2. Collective: why we are doing this and
		3. Personal: your reasons
		Focus on their 'why's': what's important for to them
		Make the purpose for the feedback attractive and compelling
		Use storytelling to explain purpose

Threat prompt/reward type	Specific feedback actions likely to create threat	To build or maintain a reward state when giving feedback
Belonging	Feedback that leaves someone out of the group Asking them to do things they can't manage Exclusion of any form Disconnecting the other from people they are close to Any action that can be perceived as discrimination	Make extra efforts to include Hear and understand their experience Foster and support their need to belong Acknowledge where there is bias, making efforts to correct this Be humble and apologetic if you have contributed to that Create collaborative actions
Success, achievement and outcomes focused	Suggest ways forward that interfere with achievement Disinterest in or failure to recognise specific successes Fail to recognise pressure, overload or too much multitasking	Problem-solve to find a way forward Create a plan for success Support with priority setting Remove barriers to success Identify meaningful successes Use and focus on data Use the feedback session as collaborative thinking time
Equality	Show that you are treating this person differently to others Expect something different from this person compared to colleagues Inconsistent across your department Dismiss their concerns about fairness	Demonstrate why this is fair, consider both the process and expected outcomes Consistent explanations to all staff Repetition of the expectation and why this is fair Take their concerns seriously Demonstrate what is said is done

Communicating Purpose
Understanding what's going on
Understanding the story of why:
the intent, high level plan, any
changes and the progress
Vision, goal, aspiration
WIIFMs, attractive
Mitigation: process information

Support & Acknowledgement
COMES FIRST WHEN EMOTION
Listen & support, understanding,
empathy, compassion
Offer help, needs time & space
Leadership containment: no
'seeping'

[Enhancing] Trusted Relationships
Authentic, honest, open, integrity
Fair process
People consistently treated with dignity and
respect
Everyone genuinely asked their views (and
listened to)
Recognition for what's gone before

Clear Direction & Expectations
'What and how', linked to purpose
Clear, concise, specific details, e.g.
timescale
Focus on practicalities, logistics, what's
happening, Expected outputs, steps
Info so people can make decisions & take
control

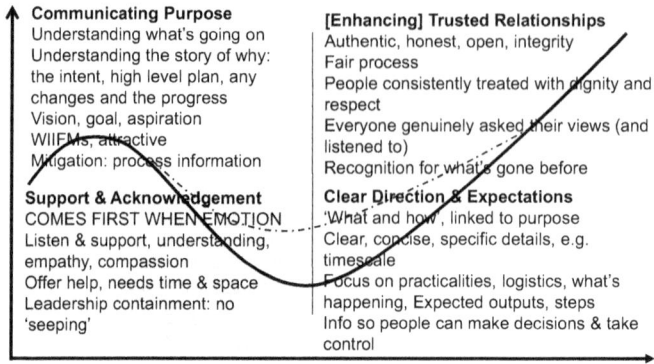

Figure 13.1 The tasks of transition that help adaptation to change and to influence

them open questions, hearing their side of the story and empathising. This may result in you offering support and help with what you are wanting. It also enables people to hear those expectations, so having this more Nurturing Parent style conversation first enables a tried, threatened brain to begin to hear what is expected of them, what they have not been doing well and to start to process the improver feedback

4. *The importance of enhancing the trusted relationship*: all the way through behaviours that support enhancing trusted relationships are recommended. These include showing respect, inviting contributions and suggestions, providing recognition, showing your own voluntary vulnerability and the demonstration of fairness

The GROW model is an early coaching model. It is now commonly used as a framework for coaching conversations in the workplace and I think it's also a helpful way of structuring a difficult conversation. It's especially helpful for feedback by beginning to explore why someone is not performing and, in later conversations, can show where to introduce more firmness. It contains a set of questions that I have developed into what I call a '2-way GROW' that indicates when and what the feedback-giver can do and say so that their views and needs are included.

GROW stands for Goal, Reality, Options and Way Forward.

Goal: in a feedback conversation you are the person setting the objectives and purpose for the meeting. However, you can also ask what the other wants from the session and whether they have any other more important goals. Together you can agree what success looks like and set some boundaries for the meeting, for example, by asking 'What do you need from me in this meeting? Then you follow this up with your needs.

Reality: in this section of the conversation you find out what has been happening. It's useful to treat this section as solving the puzzle of why something has not been happening the way you expected or why difficulties have arisen. This section is very much focused on hearing and understanding the other person's 'reality'. It is considered the most missed out section of unsuccessful feedback conversations. Helpful questions here include:

- What's really been happening?
- What's been going on?
- Has this goal been realistic for you?
- Help me understand ...
- What have you done to fix it?

Once you've exhausted your curiosity and have a better understanding of what's been going on, the 2-way GROW allows for your reality to be introduced. Here, you explain your perspective, remembering to use Free Child, describing how it feels and has been like for you and you give your view of the reality. Don't forget to ask questions about how this is received. This is not telling or judging the other, this is a collaborative exercise for you both to understand where the other is coming from.

Options and obstacles: there comes a natural point, or maybe one dictated by time, where you move collaboratively to collecting and working through different options, this incudes talking about what may get in the way. Useful questions to include here are:

- What are some ways you/we could approach this?
- What are both creative and realistic ways forward?
- What can we do about obstacles?
- My expectations are ... What do you think of these?
- What are the advantages and disadvantages of the various options?

Way forward: in this last segment of the conversation some agreement about what is required next. In this model, you come to this agreed action through asking questions. Here are some possibilities:

- Which option is your best choice?
- What's the first step?
- What else do you need, including from me, to make this happen?
- On a scale of 1–10, how committed are you to this plan?

- What support do you need?
- What will you and I do?
- Or (*in extremis*) I need you to do …, like this … (you'll need to explain your reasoning for this)

13.7 Preparing and planning feedback conversations

If you've been reading this and wondering how on earth you can change your feedback-giving practice, then this is the section for you. From the research I've been reading (for example, Hougaard and Carter, 2022; Porter, 2019) the single most frequently occurring predictor of the failure of feedback to have impact is that it's not planned. Preparing feedback is crucial to its success. This isn't just thinking about what you'll say, it's creating the right environment, having data to make clear your points and considering how to individualise your approach. It's also preparing yourself for the experience and managing your own threat responses.

I like Jennifer Porter's four step Intentional Planning Method (2019) for giving feedback:

Step 1: be present: be aware of the impact and the environment. This is about stopping and thinking about what you are about to do, the likely impact on both you and the other person. It gets you thinking about what they need and how, including the environment you'll need to create for the feedback to be heard. Do they prefer conditional or unconditional feedback? Do they have particular threat prompts or other needs you can be aware of? Will taking them for coffee be better than booking a meeting room?

Step 2: be self-aware: how do you think you'll feel delivering this feedback? Will you be under threat too? How will this change your behaviour and speech – will it mean that you do not have the required impact despite your intent? Think about what you need to do to self-regulate: this may be increasing your social support by talking it through with a trusted colleague, maybe it's setting uninterrupted time aside so that you are well prepared or maybe you'll need some of those self-management techniques discussed in Chapter 4

Step 3: identify behavioural actions in advance: if you want to remain in the effective ego states consider how you will do this. Think about how to use all three effective ego states, especially your least used ego state as that is likely to be harder to reach under pressure. Some people find it useful to visualise how they want the meeting to go, focusing on delivery, specific words, the pace, they pick the questions they most want to ask and they prepare themselves to listen more than tell

Step 4: choose the most productive and effective behaviours. There will have been a lot to consider in this preparation activity. This is about identifying the top three actions you will need to hold on to and remember in the meeting, especially if it's emotionally charged. Write these down as reminders and have them somewhere visible

13.8 What to do when it doesn't work

When you've got to the end of the line, when the feedback isn't being heard, what then? See Chapter 14, on instilling ownership, where I look at how to stay firm and what to do in more extreme circumstances.

13.9 Self-reflection

- Do you feel a sense of dread when you give or get feedback?
- Do you give feedback to people for whom this is a threat?
- Are you using all the effective ego states when you give difficult feedback? Which one could you deliberately do more of?
- Do you give both conditional and unconditional Strokes in feedback?
- Do you tailor your feedback to individuals? Think of someone you need to give improver feedback to; in particular, consider their threat prompts and rewards needs. What will work best for them?
- Would a structure for feedback help you?
- How much do you prepare both what you want to say and how you'll say it? Think about someone you need to give feedback to, plan it using the four steps above and/or consider key questions from the GROW model to ask in the meeting

References

Hougaard, R., & Carter, J. (2022). *Compassionate leadership: How to do hard things in a human way*. Harvard Business Review Press.

Porter, J. (2019, 19 June). How to Move from Self-Awareness to Self-Improvement, *Harvard Business Review*. https://hbr.org/2019/06/how-to-move-from-self-awareness-to-self-improvement

West, T.V., Thorson, K., Grant, H., & Rock, D. (2018). Asked for vs unasked for feedback: An experimental study. *Neuroleadership Journal*. https://membership.neuroleadership.com/material/asked-for-vs-unasked-for-feedback-an-experimental-study/

14

HOW DO I INSTIL OWNERSHIP? WHAT TO DO WHEN SOMEONE IS NOT PERFORMING AS YOU NEED THEM TO

In the years following the pandemic this is the question I have been asked most. I think that this is because there was high emphasis on well-being and resilience during and just after the pandemic years: however, since then I've noticed a tension between maintaining that focus on well-being and getting the job done. This chapter presents how to be firm and fair using a specific, and very neat, method from Rasmus Hougaard and Jacqueline Carter (Hougaard & Carter, 2022) that I really rate. It showcases how to use all the three base models, the ego states, the transition cure and how to minimise threat states. It follows directly on from Chapter 13, the chapter on feedback, so I advise that you read both together. However, the chapter begins by looking at yourself: in my experience a significant part of why something has not been done is because of the way it was explained or 'sold'. I've looked extensively in this book at why other people don't engage with key messages. This may be the perception of the ineffective ego states, there may be threat states for one, the other or both inhibiting logical thinking, and I've considered resistance as a potential and natural response to any change. So, while you probably want to read a chapter about being firm with others and holding the line, I start this chapter by encouraging you to take a good look at your own behaviours before you move on to how to hold the line.

Even if you consider yourself to have great leadership skills and an exemplary feedback technique, there are times when feedback isn't heard or people decide to do things their own way. How to instil ownership, have people performing, and at the pace needed, is one of the questions I am asked most. It's not uncommon for me to hear the frustrated cry of a leader, 'I've tried everything, how do I deal with such poor performance?' Or 'How do I get them to see how important this is?' All the leaders I encounter want to do the best for and by their teams, so another question I am asked is 'I want to give them one more chance, but how should I do this?' This chapter addresses what to do to really instil ownership.

DOI: 10.4324/9781003623250-19

14.1 There's a reason for every behaviour

The first thing I suggest a leader does is to 'look beyond' to treat the situation as a puzzle to be solved. I learnt early on in my clinical psychology training that there is a reason for every behaviour and that it is my role to work out what seems puzzling. So, begin by asking yourself what all the possible reasons might be why something you've asked for is not being done or not getting done the way you want. There will be myriad possibilities; here are the most common reasons that I hear:

- What you're suggesting may seem realistic to you but unrealistic to me
- I've a lack of time, I've too much to do
- I've conflicting or unclear priorities leading me to paralysis
- I disagree, this is a bad idea
- I don't know how and I don't want to show my vulnerability as you have the power over me
- I made a mistake and I don't want you to know
- I think there is a better way, I'm waiting for a chance to explain it to you

Some of these may cause you frustration or discomfort: you may rail against the realistic point; despair as there are tools out there for people to better organise themselves; see yourself having an open door and be hurt that someone can't tell you how they are feeling or cross as you've invested in them and they still seem unable to do it. Whatever your reaction, acting out that emotion, which will show in the ineffective ego states won't help you to solve this puzzle. Step one is to manage your own reaction so that you can engage your PFC, to take a proper analytical look at what is going on. There may be some problem-solving to be done as a process isn't working, maybe there are barriers to be overcome, perhaps someone is reacting angrily or resentfully to what you've requested or it may be very clear that someone doesn't have the capability to do as you asked.

Spending time on this puzzle and taking a problem-solving approach is the starting point here.

14.2 Could it be me?

I worked recently with a CEO who was very frustrated that his top leadership group of 25 kept bringing problems, not solutions, to the priorities they'd set themselves. He wanted to explore why people weren't taking accountability, why they constantly complained about the targets set and why they didn't seem empowered to take action. On meeting him for the first time, then interviewing some of his closest colleagues, it became very clear. His language and expression were judgemental: it was all about how people weren't doing what he wanted, with a strong implication that it was their fault. He was critical of their use of the resources given and of their decision making. He was offering little support. He was adapting his emotion of frustration into blame and letting that show. He was communicating in a way that others perceived as Critical Parent and Rebellious Child, with little Nurturing Parent to help and little Free Child to explain himself. We were to run an event exploring this puzzle: the only way I could see this would work was if I could help him to have his framing, his reasoning, for the event heard from Nurturing Parent and Free Child, transforming his message from a Critical to a Nurturing Parent. Once we'd worked on his narrative it explained how frustrated he'd become and how he wanted to help everyone to excel. This helped us to explore the puzzle openly, without people hiding what they thought.

He had no idea that his style of communication was one factor causing this inertia. I see this frequently, where a leader does not think that their behaviour is causative. Another leader I coach is very passionate and finds it hard to understand why some team members are wary of her and consequently don't always give her what she's asking for. Passion can be overwhelming, another behaviour that when communicated can be misunderstood, coming across as aggressive and impatient.

Thus, another element of working out why someone isn't doing what you want is to consider whether part of that response has something to do with you, despite your good intent.

14.3 Staying firm

Instilling ownership, ensuring that someone is working on what you need, requires a firm, clear message. Hogaard and Carter (2022) researched what was needed, asking 70,000 people what worked for them. They formulated a '4Cs' model of compassionate leadership, in essence how to be both caring and firm all at the same time.

This model is based on the concept of compassion. There's been a debate running in psychology for a while now: what's most effective, empathy or compassion? If we use only empathy, we take on someone's suffering; this weighs heavily and is taxing for a leader. Empathy often feels right, we've been told is the right thing to do, but we get stuck in it. In comparison, compassion, which is defined as empathy plus action, moves us forward, stopping this empathy hijack. In leadership, too much empathy is now thought to be paralysing, preventing us from doing the hard stuff. Compassion, as it attends to the person and is action orientated, allows us to both to understand and be firm by taking action. It's a far more appropriate behavioural action for creating momentum and enhancing performance.

Hougaard and Carter's model demonstrates how compassion and action can sit together in four steps in a one–one conversation, all from the effective ego states in a way that minimises threat states.

14.4 The 4Cs model

14.4.1 Step 1: Caring presence

The starting point is being present. Imagine that you are going into a meeting with your most difficult direct report, the idea here is that you are focused and intentional before you go in, you visualise what it will be like and plan for that. You could try some form of mindfulness, even one minute of mindfulness or a brief mental break helps us to be more aware and intentional. You are entering the conversation with a clear mind.

The model also recommends some form of intentional planning, very similar to Jennifer Porter's Intentional Feedback method (2019) (see Chapter 13): you have formulated not just what you are going to say, but how: for example, what language to use or not use, which curious questions you want to ask, what is likely to have a good impact and you've worked out how to keep it concise and understandable. This is a really useful method to use when you are going to be facing a known and particularly tricky individual.

Hougaard and Carter recommend a 2–2–2 method before any difficult conversation: this is a method of awareness raising using sets of two-minute activities:

1. This starts with a two-minute pause, a break from what you have been doing,where you practise a brief mindfulness activity or even daydream (as studies show this is another good way of accessing the PFC). Here you are deliberately having a mental break
2. Then two minutes of intentional planning
3. And finally, a two-minute prioritisation activity where you order what you are going to say, checking the framing and language, and identifying the key points

They prompt us to include some key behaviours that help the beginning of difficult meetings such as curiosity, a reminder to avoid making assumptions about people and to deliberately double the ask/tell ratio. And don't forget some warmth, some social niceties and small talk at the beginning can create oxytocin and may chip away at elevated threat levels.

A summary of the 4Cs (Hougaard & Carter, 2022)

Caring presence: intentional planning: get prepared
Caring courage: preventing avoidance, being emotionally ready
Caring presence: the act of being firm
Caring transparency: making it easy to hear what you need and the art of staying firm

14.4.2 Step 2: Caring courage

This is about not avoiding. We avoid being firm or saying the hard things as we want to stay comfortable with people, but if we want to do the hard stuff we can't stay comfortable and neither can the other. Neurologically we're wired for empathy, for comfort: we far prefer to be in the reward state, where limbic system activity is low and the PFC is accessible. We often have cultures of 'niceness' that actually inhibit change and prevent accountability.

To avoid the empathy and niceness trap we need to 'feel the fear and do it, or say it, anyway'. At the same time, it's important not to let the frustration or urgency, the emotions we have, fester, as they will build or be expressed in a blaming, over-critical or accusatory way. These are essentially Adult conversations that need Nurturing Parent and Free Child to make the Adult work. Quite a challenge!

Health and social care professionals are trained in 'containment'; this is where we 'hold' our and other's emotions, we engage in emotional labour where we recognise and hold feelings back, managing difficult or potentially inflammatory emotions. This means not reacting or biting back when others respond in Rebellious Child, where they are defensive, angry or feel some-thing is unfair. To do this we need to be aware of our emotional responses and control them.

It helps if we can deliberately increase levels of self-awareness by con-sciously focusing on how we feel (see techniques to do this in Chapter 4). Then, an important way to manage our own emotions is to say them out loud: we know that telling others how we feel about a difficult situation lowers emotional intensity, so engage social support networks, in particular your peer network, before you go into an emotive conversation. This is another use of the Free Child ego state, explaining how we feel helps us to access the Nurturing Parent and Free Child ego states.

Beware, if your social support is someone in your team and this firm con-versation is with another of your direct reports, you run the risk that you will be seen to have favourites, which will set off those with Equality threat prompts and start a contagion effect where that sense of injustice trickles down. It's important to line up a debrief call with a peer colleague, mentor or peer coach after a particularly difficult situation, or, for introverts, perhaps have some quiet time to process things.

Hougaard and Carter point out that we need to get used to being cour-ageous in emotional situations: one way to do this is to set up a pattern of having a deliberately courageous conversation every day, not, as we've seen, in a brutal way but a conversational way, using all three effective ego states. We'll avoid less if we get used to doing this regularly and our own fear and threat will decrease.

14.4.3 Step 3: Caring candour

This is where the firmness comes in. This step is the essence of Hougaard and Carter's compassionate leadership and the part where the guidance on difficult conversations has changed most, as this method encourages us to be direct, but not brutal, early on in the difficult conversation. It's important to say what it is you have been concerned or frustrated about. Here are some guidelines about how to do this well, to stay out of Critical Parent or Rebellious Child, limit resistance and stop the situation moving towards a conflict loop:

1. After the social niceties and asking some curious questions as outlined in caring presence, it's important to come to the point quickly and say what needs to be said. Do this soon, use well prepared intentional language, keep it short and concise. This isn't about speaking the truth in an unguarded way, it's not brutal honesty or an unguarded thought download. Severe candour without care creates hostility, threat and stress and, whatever the intent, is highly likely to be perceived as Critical Parent. This is about being intentional and caring, not brutal. The message is delivered in a kind and direct way

2. Stating the purpose very early on is key because if we wrap messages in a long preamble or too many descriptive scenarios people lose the thread, becoming confused about the purpose. I'm working with someone who has disregarded the feedback of their manager because the manager tells so many stories and offers such a long preamble that the purpose and essence of the feedback gets lost

   It's very important that there's a reason for what you are asking or saying: remember that studies from neuroscience show that our PFC access is better when there is a clear purpose that we can align to. Using Free Child you can talk about your own needs – for example, describing why something is urgent or important for you, or why you need them to do it in a particular way. There are sections that outline communicating purpose in more detail in Chapters 4 and 12

3. Doing this quickly up front means there's time for the person to make sense of it and react: your role is to manage their emotional fallout. You are about to trigger threat: from their research Hougaard and Carter calculated a 1:6 ratio where the first sixth of the meeting is this upfront, prepared, firm narrative. The other five sixths of the meeting is the time needed to hear and understand the other as they process and potentially act out the emotions. They suggest you spend considerable time after stating your firm expectation or feedback in Nurturing Parent. It's the time needed for their brain to get back to PFC thinking. You are likely to experience dissonance here, they have entered the bottom left-hand side

of the transition curve, the strongly emotional quadrant (see Figure 13.1). Your job is to use the support and acknowledgement task of transition to help them to the reorganisation phase, the bottom right-hand quadrant, where they can think about what to do and assess their choices

One of my coachees gave me a great example recently: she needed to performance manage someone. It was a very tense conversation where she needed the other to do something very differently, when she brought this up, they blamed her, called her incompetent, it was all her fault. 'I'll fight this decision' they said. She took their dissonance, was quiet and contained: she listened, she spent rest of the session hearing their concerns in Nurturing Parent while at the same time holding firm. When they met again two days later, she was expecting this over again, but they were calmer and had moved on. The process of caring candour allowed this shift and transition in her direct report to occur.

14.4.4 Step 4: Caring transparency

The 4Cs method is all about simplification, where clarity is considered a kindness. Short crisp messages are needed throughout the interaction, these require preparation to be clear and concise, to help a threatened brain absorb information. Too much overload, a preamble or a long story gets lost and can increase the sense of foreboding, thereby increasing threat. From an ego state perspective this is what and how you communicate information from the Adult ego state: remember that communicating this ego state with emotion or judgement negates its impact.

Above all you hold firm, you do this by staying in the effective ego states, particularly Nurturing Parent, resisting the natural reciprocal pull to the ineffective ego states (Critical Parent, Rebellious Child and Compliant Child). Most of the time you stay quite quiet: your body language and words show you understand, you ask questions to draw out their narrative and perspective. But, when challenged, you stay firm. This means repeating the key message about what you expect or need or what your decision is, all statements that this method urges you to have prepared in advance. You bring no new information into this section.

Instead of agreeing with their view you can express gratitude to the person for speaking out, you can commend them to others, demonstrating that it's good to speak up and out.

Checking what people actually hear is important too, as we lose things in translation. It's another of the recommended activities to do in that remaining five sixths of the meeting, after delivering the difficult message. You can ask them questions, be curious, listen and hear, all Nurturing Parent activities. You don't have to agree but this is the kind and empathic thing to do, just don't get locked in the empathy trap and don't bring any new information.

There's a great question here: 'What are the good reasons why this won't work?' Questions like this focus on logic and move away from the emotional position (see the GROW model in Chapter 13 for similar questions).

There is one exception: hold firm unless they say something compelling. They may have a good reason for what they've done, or not done, or have a good idea, one that is worthy of attention. Since these conversations generally come at the end of the line, after coaching and the more usual methods of feedback have been attempted, it's unlikely, but not impossible, that something new will come up. Also, if needed, admit it if you discover you are wrong: this is an example of being vulnerable, you can them for ask for help; overall, you are behaving with integrity.

14.5 Changing the person

I worked for a very wise mentor, Mark Hamlin,[1] whose answer to the question 'What can I do when someone is not performing?' was, 'If you can't change the person, then you need to change the person.' What he meant was, ask yourself if you have worked hard enough, on yourself, to offer the other person different and compelling behaviours to which they could respond reciprocally. If you have behaved differently and have received a different, more effective reciprocal response back, then you have enabled them to perform better. However, these techniques aren't foolproof, they don't always work and sometimes we come across people whose capabilities or behaviours don't change. We've given them ample opportunity to do something differently and that hasn't happened. Mark would say, 'Give it three goes, adapt your behaviour three times and if that doesn't work then it's time to change the person'.

This means managing the person out. This is why there are formal policies in place to help you when you reach the end of the line. Whatever you think of these and your HR department, which, in my experience, works valiantly to support you, they are there for you to use in these moments.

There are many consequences of not tackling long-term poor performance, insubordination or poor workplace behaviours. Ruth Wageman, who researches and writes about team effectiveness, cites not managing out the poor performer as one of the key factors that undermines not just team performance but team cohesiveness and psychological safety too (Wageman, 2021). (See more on this and Ruth's work in Chapter 16 on creating effective teams).

14.6 Brutal feedback does not instil ownership

If the process and techniques described in this chapter seem too soft for you, then consider this: the more brutal the feedback and the lack of time for emotional processing edges you closer to the conflict loop and embeds you more on the bottom left-hand side of the transition curve, the place, where *in extremis*, sabotage and sickness lie. You are far more likely to be on the receiving end of a grievance or complaint if you don't reign in your Critical Parent or Rebellious Child. You have choices: to look beneath, to look within yourself to see what your role has been, to offer compassion and work on how you are firm – these are the humane performance management behaviours of an effective early twenty-first century leader.

14.7 Self-reflection

Consider someone in your team who is not performing well:

- What's going on for them? What lies beneath? Is there some reasonable explanation for their performance?
- Could it be you? Could your communication be coming across as Critical Parent, or Rebellious Child, especially if that's not your intent?
- How could you use intentional planning methods to approach such difficult conversations?
- Are you firm enough? Have you simplified your expectation or concern so that it can be easily heard? Do you repeat this? Is it coming across in Adult, with emotion and judgement removed?
- Are you being compassionate? Are you being Nurturing Parent and listening enough? Are you supporting and acknowledging someone to come to terms with their needed transition?
- Is it time to change the person? Have you done absolutely everything you can?

Note

1 (M. Hamlin, personal communication) I worked with Mark, founder and Chair of the ORGroup at Organisation Resource, for 11 years between 2005 and 2016

References

Hougaard, R., & Carter, J. (2022). *Compassionate leadership: How to do hard things in a human way*. Harvard Business Review Press.
Porter, J. (2019, 19 June). How to Move from Self-Awareness to Self-Improvement, *Harvard Business Review*. https://hbr.org/2019/06/how-to-move-from-self-awaren ess-to-self-improvement
Wageman, R. (2021, 9–10 May). Six conditions for team effectiveness: The science and art of great teams. Paper presented at the Psychological Society Special Group in Coaching Psychology Conference, 2021.

15

HOW CAN I BE HEARD? THE PSYCHOLOGY OF 'VOICE'

This is a very important chapter for three reasons. First, finding yourself without voice is sadly a very common and stressful position to find ourselves in at work that requires careful consideration. Second, because in this chapter I offer you a methodology not just for finding your voice but also for analysing any relationship you are in that you want to improve. I introduce behavioural stakeholder analysis, a simple method that helps you to use the key diagnostic models and tools so far. Only attempt a behavioural stakeholder analysis if you have read the chapters on ego states, threat and reward prompts, the transition curve and Strokes, although you can include any descriptive tool that helps you to understand the impact you and a colleague are having on each other. Third, I make a difficult to hear suggestion: that sometimes we can be the starting point of difficult conversations, dynamics and ultimately challenging relationships. We may be the cause of us not having voice because we haven't considered our behaviours, and their impact, enough. If we start from a critical position that is perceived as threating by another, we are highly likely not to be heard. Through a careful analysis of our own behaviours we can make more effective choices about how we are heard and engaged with. In this chapter I show you how to do this.

In psychological studies 'voice' refers to the ability to be able to say something that you want to say. Workplace studies have been showing that voicing concerns at work is shockingly difficult to do. Sarah Brooks, a researcher on 'voice', highlighted that 85% of people withhold voice at some point at work, particularly in strong, formal hierarchies and highly process-bound organisations (Brooks, 2024: Milliken et al., 2003). Reasons given are that people don't think they'll be believed, they will be wrong and it will be seen as their fault, through to where there's too much to lose and they believe there will be some form of retaliation. Such studies demonstrated that the costs of not speaking up are massive: psychologically, this leads to self-doubts, poor relationships, disempowerment, decreased motivation and discretionary effort and an increase in mental health problems. Economically, absenteeism

DOI:10.4324/9781003623250-20

Table 15.1 Types of power through inflence (source: Brooks, 2024)

Everyone	*Leaders and managers*
Referent influence: the ability to convince anyone, including those more senior, of your argument	*Legitimate influence* with the right to ask and expect, because of your position, that you can state your needs and expectations
Expert influence: being recognised as having expertise about a subject	*Reward influence*: access to valued rewards which will be dispensed in return for good performance
Informational influence: having specific information to support your requests and expectations	*Coercive power*: access to penalties or sanctions that are considered unwelcome

increases, causing a higher turnover, there's a consequent loss of skills and periods with roles unfilled, so other people's productivity is affected.

It seems the biggest factor enabling us to speak out is power. Workers who perceive they have power are more likely to speak up. It's therefore important to remember that, at work, everyone has some form of power through influence (Table 15.1).

To have voice we need self-confidence, in particular a belief that we will be heard and a perception of psychological safety. Studies show that having a good relationship with our immediate manager helps, especially where the manager isn't verbally dominant, and having organisational voice mechanisms in place where the prevailing culture and norms encourage speaking up and out (Brooks, 2024; Chartered Institute of Personnel and Development, 2012).

15.1 How do I become heard?

The first thing to do if you are not being heard is to consider why. Perhaps there are some of the dynamics in place that were mentioned above: power, no formal mechanisms to be heard, and so on. It's important to consider the risks. If there is a particular relationship within which you are not being heard then maybe that's worthy of some investigation and diagnosis; the process outlined below will help you to decide whether to speak out and how.

15.2 Behavioural stakeholder analysis

A behavioural stakeholder analysis is a structured method that helps you to make effective behavioural choices as it breaks down what is going on. This particular form of analysis uses all three base models and tools plus the threat and reward prompts and the psychology of recognition. It is, therefore, important to have read Chapters 1–3, plus 5 and 10 before you attempt this.

Table 15.2 Behavioural stakeholder analysis grid

The person
My behaviours and reactions
My impact
My choices

This behavioural stakeholder analysis tool (Table 15.2), takes the form of a grid, mapped on to a single page, where you collect data about your own and your colleague's behaviour and psychological state and the impact that you are having on each other. This analysis enables you to carefully consider the choices you have and the likely impact these will have on the other, and ultimately you, in those circumstances.

1. *The person*: think about someone you want to work better with or be heard by, simply record that person's name and their role on the grid. Note if there is a power difference and whether they are under any particular pressure or threat, even at home (if you know)
2. *My behaviours and reactions*: consider the following and record:
    * Which ego state am I in with them when we interact?
    * Are any of my threat prompts activated? What am I experiencing?
    * What impact are they having on me? What are my reactions?
    * Which tasks of transition am I offering?
3. *My impact*: then think about this the other way around and record:
    * What impact do I think I have on them?
    * Which ego states responses do I observe when we interact?
    * Where are they on the transition curve? Are they in the bottom left-hand side, the most difficult place to be?
    * Am I prompting any of their threats?
4. *My choices*: finally, as you work through the matrix, consider what you could do to improve this relationship
    * Which ego state/s could I enact more of or less of and how? Especially:
        * Nurturing Parent: can I find more about what's going on for them and potentially help them?
        * Free Child: can I be more open and honest about what's going on for me and why I'm reacting as I am?
        * Adult: what facts or data are they missing and how can I explain those calmy and succinctly?
    * Can I build and increase reward states for either of us? How?
    * Can I give more, less or different strokes? Which one?

- Which tasks of transition could I be using and in what order in order to influence more effectively? In particular, could I be explaining my purpose more?
- Is any of this too risky? What's the evidence for these risks?
- Is there anyone else I can draw in to help me?

5. *My overview*: finally, looking at the whole grid, what does this tell you about what's going on for the two people here – remember you are both human and most likely you both have good intent. What does this formulation suggest about your choices? Now decide what you will do

Table 15.3 An example of a behavioural stakeholder analysis

The person: my direct report: they are not doing what I need or expect and are causing me problems

---

My behaviours and reactions
I am now in CP, I didn't start out like that. At first, I wanted to understand and asked them loads of questions about their approach. However, they are not doing what's in their objectives, they constantly challenge me and do the opposite of what I ask. At first, I was genuinely curious, no threat, lots of NP – my biggest ego state. Over time, I'm cross, as this isn't fair and they are risking our outcomes. I've become more and more under threat, I recognise the bottom left of transition. My behaviours are short with them, I dread seeing them, I ruminate about what they will do next. I talk about them with my boss. I've withdrawn recognition and am telling them what to do, I'm no longer so interested in their response. I can see I'm now a CP

My impact
I'm clearly not having a good impact and, thinking about it, I never was. I think they found my curiosity and desire to understand annoying. They found me indecisive and unclear from the get-go. Over time, I think they've become increasingly frustrated with me, I'm constantly getting RC responses. I observe them at the bottom of the curve too: they are bad-tempered, clearly unhappy

---

My choices
I've been thinking about how I use my Adult with them and realise I use loads of NP and FC as I'm always talking about what's going on for me and why things are important. But I think they need more clarity, more decisiveness, more reasons for things. That's their style. I think they find someone like me annoying and taking up too much of their time, so I've become an annoying threat. In particular, I could use more Adult, they need more clear direction linked to purpose. I can rely on my boss to help me, I've been moaning to her and she has been trying to get me to think more tactically about managing them and I've said I could handle it my usual way. That hasn't worked, so, to work better with them, I need to experiment with changing how I communicate with them. I also don't think saying sorry or being grateful for their patience will work either: they like factual Strokes and actions, so I need to get on with doing that more

---

CP = Critical Parent; NP = Nurturing Parent; A = Adult; FC = Free Child; RC = Rebellious Child and CC = Compliant Child.

15.3 Working with allies to influence up

The final question on the behavioural stakeholder analysis tool is: 'Is there anyone else I can draw in to help me?' This is a key question, as many people holding a position or strong view, especially in a strong hierarchy, are unlikely to be moved by a single person's view. Humans are far more likely to change their position when influenced by a majority. This is the world of group dynamics.

I've seen this form of allyship work on many occasions. One frustrated member of a team makes an angry riposte to the leader: this is heard as a threat, perceived as coming from the ineffective ego states and receives a matching reciprocal response, usually some criticism or put-down. I've seen that same person regroup, go to talk with their allies and come back with a carefully thought-out influencing strategy that involves like-minded colleagues all playing their part: I've observed that this second approach has always been more successful.

15.4 Are you making an ineffective start?

Be honest with yourself, are you the person who starts the ineffective interchange? Are you wanting to be heard but start by communicating from Critical Parent or Rebellious Child? There's a hard to hear truth here: if we start from a critical position, Critical Parent, or are resentful or petulant from Rebellious Child, we are highly likely to not be heard, and, worse, we're far more likely to be ignored or castigated as the bad person.

Two common starting positions that I frequently hear when someone wants to be heard are, 'I'm waiting for them to change their behaviours – why should I start when this is their fault', and 'I have a right to be heard'. The other person may well be in the wrong, have behaved unjustly, is even a bully or occupies a privileged position. However, the truth here is that if you behave ineffectively, creating threat for them, you will not be heard or effectively engaged with. I've got into trouble a number of times for suggesting this: I've been accused of suggesting people 'cover' their distress or strong views, that I'm encouraging poor behaviours. That's not my intent. These situations are conflict loops, where we are in threat states and wherever we choose to behave rebelliously, with resistance, resentfully pushing back or criticising the other, then, because of the mechanics of conversations and how threat works in the brain, we will still not be heard, despite how right we may be. Remember that Obama quote: 'change will not come if we wait for some other person or some other time. We are the ones we've been waiting for. We are the change that we seek' (BarackObama.com, 2008). This means that if we want to change someone's behaviour, we need to change our own behaviour first.

Table 15.4 Berne's life positions (Berne, 1962)

I'm OK – You're OK	I'm OK – You are not OK
This is the healthy mindset position	*This is judgement*
Nurturing Parent, Adult and Free Child all accessible	You are and will be perceived as Critical Parent
Outcomes – effective reciprocal responses	Outcomes – ineffective reciprocal responses, Rebellious Child, Compliant Child and Critical Parent all likely
I am not OK – You are OK	**I'm not OK – you are not OK either**
This is the compliant position	*This is the hopeless or conflicted position*
You will be in Compliant Child with a simmering Rebellious Child not far away	Both will be using ineffective communication
Outcomes – the other likely to continue to be Critical Parent	Outcomes – more Critical Parent, Rebellious Child and Compliant Child

One more model from TA is the life positions grid, which explains that our mindset going into a conversation dictates how we end up (Berne, 1962) (Table 15.4).

By making a massive effort to occupy the I'm OK – You're OK position we can turn situations around. This needs us to be curious about the other, honest about ourselves and clear about what's needed. Such conversations need to be carefully planned; intentional planning techniques help us with this (such as Jennifer Porter's four step Intentional Planning Method (2019) in Chapter 13). Similarly, the chapter on influencing (Chapter 12) reminds us that, in very difficult situations, listening more than speaking is an incredibly important strategy. This way we learn more about why someone is behaving the way they are and what motivates them, which gives us more choices about what to do.

15.5 What to do when you've tried and are still not heard

Not all influencing works. Some people remain resolute, perhaps because they've decided this is a battle they won't concede. Perhaps you've bumped into a strong value or belief of theirs or maybe you have been in conflict together for so long their Rebellious Child, manifestations of their unhappiness and anger, keeps going. Wise to-dos here are about making sensible, deep-thinking decisions about when to disengage or walk away from a situation, when you have no option but to compromise or remember what your bottom line is and decide how to stick to it. These situations require proper slow, deep-thinking: this means that you will need to get into some PFC space to work this through. These are not decisions to be taken in a threat state. Resilience strategies are needed here, and here are the four key types (see Chapter 4 for more detail):

1. *Emotional management*: you will have a repertoire of techniques that calm and soothe your limbic system. Some people can use these immediately, for others they work gradually over a few days. I have asked my colleagues how long it took them to calm down from a conflict or a situation where they were not heard, where they experienced strong emotions: the average was 36 hours! During this time it's important not to make emotionally driven decisions about what to do

2. *Social support*: as discussed in Chapter 4 on resilience strategies, some social support helps, as having this in place is the strongest correlate of workplace resilience. This is mainly because this action increases oxytocin, the neurotransmitter substance that has the biggest impact in calming the limbic system. Talking with a confidant, ideas generating with a mentor, seeking advice, seeking out a 'booster' and allowing others to help are all useful forms of social support in these difficult times

3. *Purpose*: getting back in touch with your purpose for being here, staying in your role and connecting with what you are trying to achieve is another key resilience factor. I've worked with people ready to throw in the towel, to walk away, who have reconnected with their purpose, this has re-engaged their PFC and allowed them to think more strategically about next steps

4. *Adaptation:* this is all about how to enable our PFC to work even in different circumstances: we need mental rest and quiet focused time to achieve this. When there, we need to be deliberately analytical and focus on solutions, not continually revisiting the injustices we are experiencing. We are planning our way out of the difficult situation we find ourselves in. This may mean choosing to use formal processes to complain, to take out a grievance or to focus on finding a new role

Some other, more in the moment, techniques that come from negotiation theory can be useful for those situations when we haven't been heard, protecting us against ineffective, reciprocal responses (Fisher & Ury, 2012). Smile and be gracious is my favourite, this is a great way of behaving well in a tense situation. Another commonly suggested tactic is to thank people for their opinions even if they haven't helped or heard. The psychology of these actions is that we are protecting ourselves from slipping into strong threat states, we are helping the other come down from limbic threat, where perhaps they can be more amenable, and we are buying time for ourselves to consider how to respond. Other choices here include regrouping and finding another time for the discussion or working on understanding more about what has just happened to feed into the next step of your decision.

It is at these times that formal processes are most used. In the end if you don't have voice, have tried everything that you can, you are being bullied and it's too risky to intervene or the person you are managing is consistently insubordinate, then these situations are what formal HR processes are for. When I worked for Mark Hamlin, Chair of The OR Group, he had a very wise saying for these situations: it went like this 'Analyse the situation three times, making wise choices about your behaviours: if these attempts don't work then you need to change the situation' (M. Hamlin, personal communication, 2010).

15.6 Self-reflection

- Have you ever withheld voice? Why? Did you come up with any strategies that eventually worked? If so, could you use those again?

If you are struggling with being heard:

- What sort of influencing power do you have?
- Would it be worth analysing a situation you are in to assess your choices? If so, use the behavioural stakeholder analysis tool
- Do you understand enough about why you are not being heard?
- Are there any allies you could work with in the situation where you aren't being heard?
- Do you think you could be part of the problem? Have you been using ineffective behaviours?
- What can you do to be resilient in this situation?
- Is it time to take some serious decisions about the situation you are in and what to do next? How can you make sure you are doing this rationally?

References

BarackObama.com (2008, 5 February). *Barack Obama speech: Super Tuesday* [Video]. YouTube. https://www.youtube.com/watch?v=8dzHDzvTfzQ&t=2s
Berne, E. (1962). Classification of positions. *Transactional Analysis Bulletin, 1*(3), 23.
Brooks, S. (2024). Coaching as a route to voice: A framework for change. *The Coaching Psychologist, 20*(1), 50–62. https://doi.org/10.53841/bpstcp.2024.20.1.50
Chartered Institute of Personnel and Development (2012, 1 March). *Where has all the trust gone?* https://www.cipd.org/uk/knowledge/reports/has-trust-gone-report/
Fisher, R., & Ury, W. (2012). *Getting to yes: Negotiating an agreement without giving in.* Random House Business.

Milliken, F.J., Morrison, E.W., & Hewlin, P.F. (2003). An exploratory study of employee silence: Issues that employees don't communicate upward and why. *Journal of Management Studies*, 40(6), 1453–1476.

Porter, J. (2019, 19 June). How to move from self-awareness to self-improvement, *Harvard Business Review*. https://hbr.org/2019/06/how-to-move-from-self-awareness-to-self-improvement

16

HOW DO I LEAD A WHOLE TEAM EFFECTIVELY?

Contemporary team psychology

So far, I've been considering what to do with individuals, especially those who present leaders with challenges, conflict and tension. A leader's role is most usually to lead a whole team: while all the models presented so far are applicable to groups, there are some particular psychological dynamics to know about when people are part of groups. This chapter starts by considering the teams we belong to and how that impacts our behaviours, I then move on to bust some myths about teams before homing in on what I consider the most important characteristics of teams to ensure they, and the people in them, thrive. To do this I consider some older, yet still relevant, research from the 'greats' such as Lencioni (2002) and Katzenbach and Smith (1993). Recently, I've become more interested in contemporary research, from the past ten years, that focuses on the importance of team structure, psychological safety and shared identity. To make all of this practical, I suggest how to audit your team's performance, give away some of my favourite team workshop activities and help you to decide when to call in a facilitator.

16.1 Primary teams

We all belong to multiple teams: we are 'team members' in families, communities and have hobbies where we spend time with others, particularly sports. Similarly, at work, we are in a team led by our own line manager, or Chair of the Board or Trustees, we have peers, we lead our own teams and we may be in various project groups, especially in matrix settings. Which team is our primary team, the one we put most of our energy into, is worthy of consideration. This depends on the prevailing environment and current priorities. It's also possible, and often necessary, to have joint primary and secondary teams. One of my coachees recently decided to sit with the team she led rather than with her leader and peers. For good reasons she was prioritising her primary team of the moment. However, her leader wasn't pleased, as she wanted to

DOI: 10.4324/9781003623250-21

see both teams have equal priority. This is the trick: having the energy to spend equal focus in more than one primary team where being with both is a rewarding experience.

16.2 Effective teams

There are multiple ways to assess effectiveness. I'm almost always asked to work with teams who have some sort of struggle, tension or thorny issue, who find themselves in the threat states when together. So, when I meet a team that is highly effective, where everyone gets on, there's healthy challenge and psychological safety as well as high productivity, I'm momentarily surprised. It's a reminder to me that there many effective teams out there. Unsurprisingly, this is a much studied topic; countless books, articles and models cover what makes an effective team, who needs to be in it with which roles and how they develop. Contemporary team psychology, research from the past ten years, has disproved some of what was thought to be true and bolstered our clarity of what factors determine an effective, productive team.

16.2.1 Models of effective teams

16.2.1.1 Myths about teams

Do you think about where your team is using the very well-known 'Forming, Storming, Norming and Performing' model of team development from Bruce Tuckman (1965)? It's a myth.[1] First, it's been shown not to be linear, where each phase doesn't need to follow the other, and second, not all teams storm, some form, norm and perform: it's so refreshing to know that. Another team myth demonstrated by Tannenbaum and Salas (2020) in their book, *Teams that Work*, is that teamwork isn't always the answer: we often place people into teams for convenience but Tannenbaum and Salas demonstrated that some work tasks and projects are better done by individuals.

16.2.1.2 Lencioni's five dysfunctions of teams

A frequently used model of team effectiveness is from Patrick Lencioni (2002). This is still considered highly valid; it includes an early description of what we now call 'psychological safety' (see Chapter 7), suggesting that effective team working begins with trust. Without this, a spiral is created, ultimately leading to poor performance. In this model:

1. In the absence of trust people are not able to be vulnerable, which translates into people not telling the truth, asking for help, not naming problems and so things go underground

2. This leads to a fear of conflict, where people protect an artificial har-mony that stifles any productive disagreement. When this happens, new ways of doing things are inhibited, new solutions to problems are less likely to be found and the ability of the group to embrace diversity of thinking and take action is diminished
3. All of this leads to a decrease in commitment, which means there's a lack of engagement or buy-in, which means people don't do as they say they'll do. They do their work in their own way, they are not doing things for the collective good but for their own good
4. This means that people become too afraid to hold each other account-able, difficult conversations cease, the BMW club (bitching, moaning and whinging) grows, the gossip is rife but underground
5. And, of course, it goes without saying that this has a massive impact on the team's collective results as now it's all about individual performance

Lencioni's model is a really good one to audit, especially on team away days, as by identifying what's missing demonstrates what a team can effect-ively work on together to improve.

16.2.1.3 Katzenbach and Smith's high performing teams

Another model that I still use to help teams think about how they can be even more effective is Katzenbach and Smith's (1993) model of team performance, demonstrating how different levels of unity have an impact on outcomes. They described:

*   Working groups, where cohesion is low with reasonable performance. These are not teams but more a group of individuals whose outputs rely on the sum of an individual's work. They don't pursue collective outputs that require joint effort. Members of a working group interact primarily to share information and practices that enable them to act within their own sphere of responsibility
*   A pseudo team is neither cohesive nor productive. This group of people are focused on individual efforts above the collective, not delivering any joint benefit. This may be a particularly dysfunctional team where safety and trust is low, or a group of people who have not taken the time to work out why they exist and how to work together
*   A potential team is a new team that is moving in the right direction but hasn't yet established collective accountability. The team will need more clarity on purpose, goals, work-products and a common working approach to increase performance
*   A real team is a team that performs, members are equally committed and hold themselves mutually accountable for their common purpose, goals and working approach

- According to Katzenbach and Smith (1993), who coined the description 'highly performing team', this is where members are deeply committed to one another's personal development and success. They suggest that such teams are transitory. They do not necessarily exist for long enough to achieve this level of performance and are always subject to personnel changes

In their seminal book, *The Wisdom of Teams* (1993), they defined the characteristics of all these types of team. However, while these descriptions of team types have stood the test of time, more recent research has shed light on which specific characteristics of teams are needed for success.

16.3 New learning from contemporary team psychology

There are two newer facets of effective team functioning that have emerged in the psychology literature in the past ten years, 'psychological safety', described in detail in Chapter 7, which, in this context, is how we feel in the team, and 'shared identity', which is what we collectively believe. This latter concept comes from the work of Haslam et al. (2020): influenced by modern social psychology, their focus is not on individual behaviour but is all about how groups and teams collectively believe and then behave. For example, their work with UK emergency services found that, in crises, people step up, perform well, act in orderly ways and are supportive of others displaying solidarity behaviours. This occurs because people identify with the group, leading to coordination between group members. They call these solidarity behaviours 'shared identity', where each individual believes they are part of something, a common group, where they are connected to others through a shared purpose and experience. When we lack shared identity, when we don't believe in the reasons for solidarity, we stop adhering, we don't support those around us.

Haslam and his colleagues go further, describing this as dangerous, because when we aren't in solidarity, we're alone and then we then find other people to be alone with, so we form splinter groups. Such 'in and out groups' can become powerful conflicting forces, not helpful in a team that is meant to be cohesive. So, we need people to think of teams as 'we places', not 'I places'. In successful teams there is a strong belief in the purpose of being in the team.

16.4 Characteristics of highly performing teams: the Pearlman–Shaw model

I have drawn my own model of effective teams' characteristics from four contemporary research sources:

The right skills, people, structure	Shared and clearly understood purpose	Clear roles and responsibilities
Certain behavioural & psychological ways of being together that create unity & cohesiveness	The scaffolding: a supportive context	Effective leadership

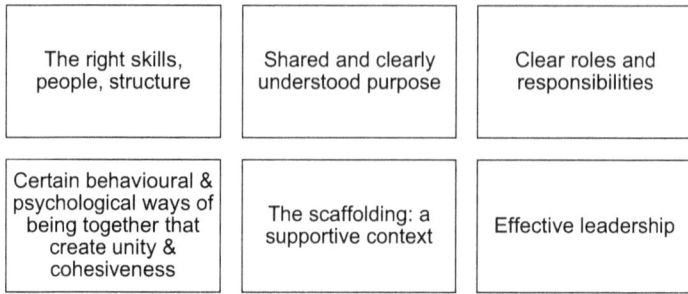

Figure 16.1 Characteristics of highly performing teams: The Pearlman-Shaw model

1. Amy Edmondson's *The Fearless Organization* (2019), her work on psychological safety
2. Haslam et al.'s *The New Psychology of Leadership* (2020), described above
3. Tannenbaum and Salas's 2020 book on their research, *Teams that Work*
4. The '6 Conditions of Teams' model from (Hackman & Wageman, 2012) that I first learned about when I heard Ruth Wageman speak at a conference I attended in 2021

My model is all about how people work together, allowing each person's brain to be in a reward state as much as possible; we want effective team members to be able to support each other to use their brains well. This means being able to sustain their own and others' resilience. This is not about always behaving wonderfully well but understanding enough about each other to support and help when others are struggling. It's being able to create inclusive environments characterised by effective ego state behaviours where people can use all of the four transition tasks to help each other through the inevitably difficult times.

The starting point is to create the right environment for a team.

16.4.1 The right structure, people and skills

Ruth Wageman focuses on what is required for interdependency. If a needed task, project or set of outcomes requires little dependency, why form a team if cooperation doesn't matter. Where people can work as a 'working group', interacting, sharing information and practices so that they can act within their own sphere of responsibility, then you don't need team players. Why would anyone want to attend a team meeting if half the agenda has nothing to do with them? Team working by nature is interdependent, so the starting point is bringing people together who really do have a need to work together. If you have four people in a team of eight who do quite independent tasks, don't have them as core team members, create different, parallel structures for them. A 'forced' structure, where people believe what they are there for is not linked, is thought to be a key reason for team tension, as shared identity will be lower.

Next consider the people and their skills. Capability is, of course, important, an effective team has the right people, with the needed mix of skills and abilities. These are not just technical competences, team fit, the style the team member operates with, is equally important. Nowadays, most organisations, when recruiting, look equally at personality preference as well as specialist skills. Tannenbaum and Salas (2020) note that just by adding a technical star doesn't boost performance. I've seen too many teams get excited about the 'saviour' they've just recruited but that person's personal performance drops considerably when they enter a team where they don't fit. A controversial and relatively new view about who makes the best team players, those who enable team safety to grow, are cooperative people who prefer to work collaboratively, they are low on narcissism and high on cooperation.

On a similar theme, both Tannenbaum and Salas (2020) and Wageman (2021) say get rid of toxic team mates. Threat states, conflict loops in teams, especially negativity and rudeness, leads to emotional contagion which spreads 'like the flu'. So don't hire or tolerate poor behaviours. Get rid of team derailers. This also has an impact on how teams are seen and perceived externally: Tannenbaum and Salas found that where there was more perceived cooperation in senior teams employee satisfaction and retention increased by an estimated 20%.

16.4.2 Shared purpose

There needs to be a clear reason to belong to a team that is compelling and meaningful, the group need to accomplish what is needed by their organisation in a way that requires solidarity, members working together. Importantly, this needs to be a shared belief in order to create a shared identity. The team needs to be able to differentiate itself from other teams, have a unique selling point, doing what only they can do. But teams can't operate with this alone.

16.4.3 Clear roles and responsibilities

Coupled with a shared purpose are the clear and shared goals and priorities that the members of the team are to achieve together. These need to be regularly reviewed. Next comes clear definition of roles and responsibilities where it's thought that the most important roles to identify are the decision makers. Often neglected is the agreement of role boundaries; where one person's accountability ends and another's starts (I recommend a series of RACIs[2] or role matrices to delineate these), as well as where it is required, and thereby safe, to stray into another's domain and how. Consequences

THE PSYCHOLOGY OF EFFECTIVE LEADERSHIP

need to be agreed when procedures are not followed or shared systems not used.

Remember that a brain functions well with clarity and plans, these allow us to access our PFC more. The absence of such clarity is one of the prime reasons for team tension and conflict and a breakdown in relationships. Tannenbaum and Salas (2020) found that teams who regularly discuss their roles and responsibilities, creating clarity, including how they behave, are thought to be 20% more effective than teams who don't.

16.4.4 Have 'scaffolding': a supportive context

This is all about the relationships and reputation that the team has with other teams in the same organisation or whomever they work with outside of their team. This is considered the most important characteristic by two of the research teams I've drawn from. In particular, if a team isn't supported by the rest of the organisation, isn't granted the needed resources, including staffing, budget, equipment and time, then a team will be more likely to perform poorly. The success of a team is strongly linked to whether it is recognised and supported for doing what it is doing. Teams can easily fail if they are not given the resources to thrive: in environments of shortages we naturally compete both internally and externally, then we see the Lencioni spiral of low trust and increasing conflict emerge.

This also includes the physical work environment: consider whether this is conducive to productivity. I once worked with two teams who had to work closely together, one had swanky new offices, the other worked in a mouldy damp suite of offices. How do you think that worked out?

From the original Katzenbach and Smith's (1993) high performing teams model we knew that the difference between a real team and a highly performing team was the investment in the development of the team and the people in it. This is still so. A team who has the time and space for education and training together is more likely to build trust; this is especially true if the team engages in a team development or coaching process. This is considered so important that in Ruth Wageman's six conditions model it's actually one of the six conditions.

16.4.5 A safe and enjoyable way of being together

This is what this book is all about: creating inclusive safe environments where everyone can participate and get along. All four of the authors that I follow devote a significant portion of their commentary to this characteristic, something in the past that my colleagues and I have referred to as 'teaminess'. They all identify support, sharing, curiosity, listening and understanding, the ability to speak up and be heard, gratitude, creating success and having fun together as key behaviours for team success.

There are specific findings that are notable:

- That if there is too much emphasis on this then outputs are neglected – Ruth Wageman
- This doesn't come naturally, teams need to develop this – Tannenbaum and Salas
- Doing things altogether increases shared identity – Haslam, Reicher and Platow
- The need to embrace failure together, experimenting and learning as a team – Amy Edmonson

I've included this chapter in this section of the book as I think that using all three base models are what's needed to create safe and enjoyable ways of being together. This highlights the need to behave effectively, not judging others, using the effective ego states and being mindful to use all four of the transition tasks to enable yourself and others to adjust to, and engage with, each new goal or situation, so that everyone can be in reward, not threat, states as much as possible.

Practically, creating behavioural charters for your team, and agreeing how they will be enforced are ways to set such an environment for your team. These are lists of agreed behaviours and actions that all team members will adhere to. It's a way of making the behavioural elements of team working as clear as the purpose, roles and responsibilities.

In busy task-driven environments, teams naturally neglect the space to grow the trust and psychological safety[3] needed to create an atmosphere that is safe and enjoyable. There are many ways to do this, from making sure there is some unstructured time in regular meetings to find out how people are doing and what's going on for them, asking specific questions that grow psychological safety and having regular away days with time for discussion and revision of behavioural charters and cohesion building activities (see the selection below on activities and good questions to ask on away days and Chapter 7 for more on psychological safety).

16.4.6 Leadership

Leadership of teams has always been seen as fundamental to team success. Amy Edmondson (2019) has a lot to say about how leaders can create psychological safety: they encourage people to speak out by being curious, listening and understanding challenges. They encourage experimentation taking away fear by embracing failure as learning. They show voluntary vulnerability by acknowledging that they don't know everything and they are grateful for people speaking out. Tannenbaum and Salas (2020) add that effective team leaders can deal with discord, facilitating resolution of task conflict, thereby preventing interpersonal conflict amongst team members. They favour an egalitarian, coaching style of leadership where everyone leads on something. Ruth Wageman (Hackman & Wageman, 2012, Wageman, 2021) focuses more on the leader ensuring that the structure is correct, with the team being the right size for their required interdependencies. They are the negotiator with the wider system for resources and they facilitate effective team performance by rewarding success and ensuring there's minimal competition between members.

Haslam et al. (2020) add the importance of the leader creating fairness by procedural justice. They do this by focusing on 'we', the whole, not singling out individuals. The leader is consistent, they treat people using the same systems and processes; for example, they emulate fairness by not neglecting to discipline one person when they've pulled another up on their performance. They are good at Free Child, they can explain their personal purpose for their actions. They involve the team in decisions, providing the opportunity for redress, for voice, hearing what is brought. Haslam and colleagues' research showed that people tend to view a situation as fairer when leaders are transparent about why they are resolving a dispute or why they are bringing in a new policy. Similarly, team members are more likely to view an interaction as fair when the leader shows a genuine and impartial concern for the interests of all the parties involved.

All of this requires what's known as 'servant leadership', where the leader sees themselves as the facilitator of everyone else's success. The leader needs to contain their frustrations and anxieties, making sure they have adequate social support and resilience mechanisms to be able to hold this position.

16.5 Auditing characteristics of highly performing teams

These six characteristics are easy to audit. Simply ask each team member to score how well they think the team performs on each factor. This can be done live in a team away day or before, using a Google form, where you present the results at the session. Each characteristic can be discussed with focus on what could be done to improve, culminating in agreeing actions to take forward. It's important not to get drawn too much into what's wrong as this takes the focus off improvements.

16.6 Team activities for building team relationships

As you've seen, arranging dedicated time for the team to spend together is considered crucial for effective team performance. Of course, you need time together to go over business plans, re-do and revise strategy and consider priorities and timelines. Attending to team relationships is important too, in order to agree expectations of each other, explore potential tensions, to understand each other more and to have fun. Here are some of my favourite activities for different team needs.

For a newly formed team:

- Spend time not just on the team's purpose but why each person is here and what they want from the journey you are about to embark on
- Work on roles, responsibilities and boundaries
- Talk overtly about what behaviours matter to people in the team and use this as the basis for your team charter
- Ask: what do we need to know about you to work effectively with you and what do you need to know about me?

To grow psychological safety:

- Ask how we are doing as a team: what is working well, what less well? Have everyone talk in turn. Follow with a sense making or consolidation activity, a 'so what does this mean' conversation before moving to action planning
- Similarly ask: what gives me energy and drains my energy in this team?
- Celebrate success at every meeting
- Ask and discuss 'what keeps you awake at night'?
- Have 'blooper' (failure) of the week in every team meeting: this way talking about failure and learning from it becomes an acceptable norm
- Ask 'what are we missing'? Routinely asking this question helps to avoid confirmation bias and to enable those who have been quiet or uncomfortable to speak up. This works best if gratitude and appreciation are expressed when there is tension
- Implement blameless post-mortems; these shift focus from blame to learning, 'look what/how much we've learned'. Have team rules that prohibit and call out blame, shame or attack

16.7 Models to use to aid personal understanding

There are plenty of models to use that help teams understand each other better, especially to understand why members are reacting as they are. These are conversations that deepen understanding and mean that we are more likely to take more effective behavioural choices in our relationships with each other. Most of my favourites appear in this book:

- The seven threat prompts and reward needs are a great way of understanding what frustrates and upsets people and, conversely, what helps them to thrive (Chapter 5)

- Considering where people are on the transition curve, this helps to understand the pace and nature of change in, for example, a project or towards KPIs and what individual needs are at any point in time (Chapter 3)
- The TA ego states, a mechanism to understand each other's communication style to prevent misperceptions
- Considering strengths and who has which – to ensure there's someone for all team roles and you're getting the best out of everyone (Chapter 17)

There are hundreds a books and tools with great activities and questions for teams to work through. Have confidence in those you've used before and read around for new ones.

16.8 To have fun

- Book social time, meals together, host quizzes
- Get outside: treasure hunts, sports, team walk and talks
- Treats – these depend on budget and personal preferences and are a great way of creating reward states

16.9 Using psychometric tests

You'll note that there's little mention of psychometric tests in this book. MBTI (Myers Briggs), Insights, DiSC and SDIs, to name a few, are popular with teams as they show personality type or preference, conflict style and many more facets of behaviour, all predicting how your colleagues will respond to you and how to get the best from each other. Swapping personal insights helps to create wider understanding of individual, then collective, needs. I don't use these very often, the simple reason being that the methods above get us to the needed conversation far quicker than the time spent administering the psychometric tool, understanding and disseminating reports and results, then remembering what the tool is telling you. I've passed many hours with teams who've done the MBTI, which begin with everyone remembering what their letter combination means, then how this translates into behaviour. In the same time we can have had meaningful conversations, perhaps using two of the frameworks in this book, helping to enhance understanding and creating workable solutions to move forwards.

Whatever method you choose, you are finding the best way of having the team conversation you need, usually one you don't often have the time for, that will take you in the needed direction. It's important to keep these future and solutions-focused to avoid falling into the 'groan' zone or triggering too much threat. Make sure everyone goes away with one or two personal commitments as well as any needed team actions.

16.10 External facilitation

Have it externally facilitated when:

- There's tension and disagreement
- There's a thorny problem that's hard to solve
- The team want to learn together where no one has the expertise
- The leader wants to hear about what's going on and contribute their own thoughts and feelings instead of running the session

16.11 Self-reflection

- Do you have more than one primary team? If so, how can you distribute your energy and attention equally between the two?
- How strong is trust in your team? Is a lack of trust causing Lencioni's team dysfunctions?
- What sort of team is yours? Is this the type of team you want and need it to be?
- Create a six-box grid on a page: use this to consider how strong your team is on each of the six characteristics of highly performing teams. What's good, what could be better and how?
- What do you think you could do to lead your team even more effectively?
- Have you booked you team's next away day? Select a team activity for that day

Notes

1. Contemporary team psychologists have shown that not all teams develop sequentially, many don't need to storm. See Hackman and Wageman (2005).
2. RACI is a matrix demonstrating who is responsible, accountable, consulted and informed.
3. See Helbig and Norman (2023) for lots of activities to build psychological safety.

References

Edmondson, A.C. (2019.) *The fearless organization: Creating psychological safety in the work-place for learning, innovation and growth.* Wiley.

Hackman, J.R., & Wageman, R. (2005). A theory of team coaching. *The Academy of Management Review, 30*(2), 269–287. https://doi.org/10.2307/20159119

Hackman, J.R., & Wageman, R. (2012). Foster team effectiveness by fulfilling key leadership functions. In E.A. Locke (Ed.), *Handbook of principles of organizational behavior: Indispensable knowledge for evidence-based management.* John Wiley & Sons. https://doi.org/10.1002/9781119206422.ch15

Haslam, S.A., Reicher, S., & Platow, M.J. (2020). *The new psychology of leadership: Identity, influence and power* (2nd ed.). Routledge.

Helbig, K., & Norman, M. (2023). *The psychological safety playbook: Lead more powerfully by being more human*. Page Two Press.

Katzenbach, J.R., & Smith, D.K. (1993). *The wisdom of teams: Creating the high-performance organization*. Harvard Business Review Press.

Lencioni, P. M. (2002). *The five dysfunctions of a team: A leadership fable*. Jossey-Bass.

Tannenbaum, S., & Salas, E. (2020). *Teams that work: The seven drivers of team effectiveness*. Oxford University Press.

Tuckman, B.W. (1965). Developmental sequence in small groups. *Psychological Bulletin, 63*(6), 384–399. https://doi.org/10.1037/h0022100

Wageman, R. (2021, 9–10 May). Six conditions for team effectiveness: The science and art of great teams. Paper presented to the Psychological Society Special Group in Coaching Psychology Conference, 2021.

Section VI

TWENTY-FIRST CENTURY LEADERSHIP

No leadership book is complete without a discussion of leadership, in particular what it means to lead and the context in which one leads. Usually this comes at the beginning of a leadership book. I've chosen to put this at the end as my focus has been on the psychological models needed to be an effective leader. This brief chapter considers that context and, most importantly, how to exist and thrive as a leader within it.

DOI:10.4324/9781003623250-22

17

CAN ANYONE LEAD? IF I CHANGE MY BEHAVIOURS, DO I CHANGE MYSELF?

Effective twenty-first century leadership

In the 20 years I've worked in leadership development what it means to lead has changed. In this chapter, I reflect on those observations, especially the massive shift I've seen since the pandemic. As a result, I think leaders are now expected to be all things to everyone: therapist to strategist; well-being adviser and task master. In psychological terms this is considered a 'double-bind', where we are confronted with two irreconcilable demands at the same time. Having made this point, I go on to consider how to lead within this paradigm. First, I think that knowing and being able to use and apply the three base models in this book will help. Second, I address a number of ways to scaffold and nurture your leadership abilities that I've not raised before in the book. These include how to lead as an introvert; when to seek coaching and mentoring; how to enhance your leadership strengths and confidence and a very important consideration of whether, and when, leadership is actually the right next step for you. And finally, I make a very important observation: leading is not changing yourself, it's about knowing yourself and adapting your leadership style to make even more effective behavioural choices in order to lead better.

17.1 Recent changes in leadership expectations

I've seen a huge shift in leadership requirements since the COVID-19 pandemic. Pre-pandemic I would talk about the shift from 'control and command' leadership to what's known as 'transformational' leadership, which I've taken to mean a more relational and human-focused style of leadership, where the leader needs to have a flexible style to engage different individuals to ensure followership, the act of following the leader. The tools and skills I've used for many years have helped leaders with this flexibility, the effective ego states and the transition tasks being key in my toolbox.

During the pandemic, leaders needed to pay extra attention to the well-being of team members, to ensure they soothed and calmed an anxious, frightened workforce in a high state of threat. During that time, I talked

DOI: 10.4324/9781003623250-23

with leaders more than ever before about the need for reward states, resilience and compassion.

Emerging from the pandemic, the expectation to ensure well-being has remained, coupled with an urgent need to keep organisations productive and drive innovation and survival. I've heard the current leadership era, the one in which I write in 2024, described as 'unprecedented'. According to the consultancy SMRS, expectations of leaders are higher than ever, there are more complex changes than ever before, where leadership is no longer based on position but on people skills (Nichols, 2024). Younger generations entering the workplace have very different expectations about their well-being and lifestyle, wanting a meaningful purpose at work. They are thought to crave authentic connections, open communication and expect psychological safety.

The era in which I am writing this book requires a leader to be agile: one minute to be results driven, commercially and productivity focused, then, in the very next moment, needing strong listening skills, compassion and a real openness to diversity, collaboration and co-creation. I think this is a big test for any human. Leaders need to be able to contain and manage their own resilience to do all of this, keeping their PFC working to make the best people and business decisions moment by moment. My more recent coaching and leadership programmes have a large section devoted to how to be both compassionate and firm, how to be a contained, resilient leader, managing time well and how to coach and empower, creating psychological safety, yet at the same time instilling ownership and accountability, all covered in previous chapters.

It's predicted that leaders of the future will need to add environmental sustainability to these attributes. As societal expectations change, they will need to be able to hear the voices of many and create structures that dismantle power.

I think today's leaders are in a double-bind, a state where we are enacting two opposite poles of thought or belief at the same time. Consider where to take one's own vulnerability: sometimes it's okay to share and be completely authentic: voluntary vulnerability is now thought to be a key facet of successful leadership. Yet, at other times, this is counterproductive, creating the contagion effect, where anxiety or anger is 'transmitted' through a team or system. As psychological safety isn't about comfort but about tolerating discomfort, it needs to be done consciously and sensitively. How do leaders make the decision about when to do what and how? These moments need the PFC to be accessible, to have good decision making at your fingertips, an agile and bespoke approach to each of your team members where you have got to know them well and good use of the effective ego states. In other words, today's great leaders need to be able to use the three core models in this book. These will help you to make those complex, on the spot decisions about your behaviours and your leadership actions.

This final chapter considers some other facets of effective leadership that will help in this double-bind world of leadership.

17.2 Have someone to talk with – coaching and mentoring

In Chapter 4, I noted the importance of social support as essential for work-place resilience. There are many forms of workplace social support: two are mentoring and coaching, both of which can be internal or external to your organisation. These are experiences that are wholly focused on you, where you talk about workplace successes and challenges. Mentoring is more about receiving advice from someone who has had similar or related experiences to you, whereas coaching is about having the time and space to think about what to do to be even more effective. This may be an open, deep, far-reaching conversation and/or, in the way I coach, using models and tools to help. The point here is that in a double-bind world, where so much is expected, it's vital to have the space to process, reflect, think, decide and learn new skills.

The success of coaching and mentoring, indeed any form of talking support, is very simple: it's about having resonance with the person you talk with. Be prepared to talk with a few people to work out who feels right for you to spend time with. That 'fabulous' coach your colleague worked with may seem patronising and shallow to you. It's a very personal choice. When your organisation has an internal offer, think carefully about confidentiality; don't discount reverse mentoring, working with someone younger, from a different area or less skilled than you, as there's plenty to be learnt from people with a different take on leadership.

17.3 Do you really want to lead? What to do when someone isn't suited to leadership

When I started work, being a leader in few years' time was the accepted convention; it's where success seemed to lie. I think this expectation still exists and it's certainly supported by many pay scales. The trouble is, you may be very successful in your chosen field but lack the skills or ability to be a leader, especially one that needs to be both relational and firm – that's a real art. The starting point is to be very honest with yourself: do you have the aptitude, the emotional intelligence, the adaptability and the growth mindset to take this on?

I wouldn't have written this book if I didn't believe that leadership can't be learnt. I'm pretty sure I was a mediocre leader in my first leadership role in the NHS in my early thirties. I had a lot to learn to move from what I now see as a control and command mindset to how I've led more recently. I've seen countless leaders transform to be able to be both compassionate and firm and be followed to the hilt by their teams, so it can be done.

You may have a reportee who is ambitious but you don't think they will be suited to leadership. They may have poor social and relational skills and rub people up the wrong way. With the right training, coaching and mentoring I've seen those people evolve into highly effective leaders. On the other hand, I've also seen enormous resources pumped into supporting someone to effect-ively lead and those efforts not working. My advice, repeated in Chapters 14 and 15, is to give it three really good efforts and if these supportive attempts don't make much of a difference, then it's time to discuss alternatives. As Ruth Wageman (2021) reminded me, the success of teams can hinge on having the right people, particularly the right leader. I think she's right: so, if leadership is not for you, then find another way of progressing that is mean-ingful to you.

Sometimes I've seen a leader who is unable to lead in one environment, as their leadership style doesn't suit that culture or set of people, be highly effective in another. I think the learning here is to have the courage to move on quickly before your confidence declines too far; this way you can recover and thrive elsewhere.

17.4 Being kind to yourself – what to do when you are beating yourself up

I meet too many leaders who are very hard on themselves; they worry they've said the wrong thing or they've offended someone, they are concerned the paper they submitted to a meeting wasn't good enough, they think not enough effort was given to a particular task or where an error has been made that they were responsible for, they can't let this go. I'm a great believer in taking responsibility for our actions, so in the first place I have my coachees think about the learning they've made in these situations. I don't let them off the hook, as if some negative impact has been caused, I believe we have a duty to acknowledge this, put it right, to make reparation and apologise. I think that these self-doubts can be healthy – without them we can enter a temporary state of narcissism (a real state common in leadership, as described by Owen and Davidson in 2009) where we absolve ourselves of our actions, don't learn and continue to have a negative, unhelpful impact on others, meaning that conflict loops become real and we do damage.

However, I also believe that we can beat ourselves up too much. A leader I worked with recently who was highly prone to negative ruminations and self-doubt managed this by deciding to take her negativity 'lightly'. She paid attention to her spiralling thoughts, training herself to keep these in the back of her mind, not giving them attention. This was her way of keeping her PFC and her deep thinking available.

When negative thoughts dominate there are accepted ways of managing these: the section on doing this in Chapter 4 suggests training your brain to always be asking yourself the question, 'What's the evidence for this?' Other schools of cognitive science use 'defusion' techniques to manage thoughts. After all, we have thousands of thoughts at once, most of which don't come to conscious awareness. Understanding that the negative thought we've just had is one of many possible thoughts but has only come to consciousness as there is an emotional link to something in the past doesn't mean it's relevant now. It's an automatic, unhelpful thought. Defusion helps to put this in perspective by focusing on other more useful, relevant thoughts instead or minimising that thought so we don't pay it so much attention. Examples of this may be singing the thought to a song or imagining it as a cartoon, both of which give the thought less cognitive power over you, or changing the narrative to be more appropriate for the current situation. These methods come from Acceptance and Commitment Therapy (ACT). Google this if you want more information.

17.5 Using your strengths – the positive psychology approach to leading

Psychologists are divided in many areas, one of which is between those who take a positive psychology approach compared to those who look at deficits in behaviours and development. Martin Seligman, the very well-known American psychologist, began to focus on positive psychology in the 1980s. He has maintained that focusing on strengths and enhancing these is enough, we can thrive by doing what we are good at.[1] Strength-based leadership is a big thing: you may have done Clifton Strengths, Strengthscope or the free, most validated psychometric in the world, Values in Action (https://www.viacharacter.org). These identify your top 5–10 strengths and your 5–10 least used strengths (another way of saying your weakest areas).

In positive psychology, instead of working on those lower strengths, which is what the deficit model does, strengths-based leadership has you using your strengths in different ways and finding others to do what you are not so good at. We know that people who do this, who express and enhance their strengths, are more engaged, have better resilience and are more productive. The idea is that you optimise strengths: for example, if you have strengths of hope, gratitude or perseverance, then focusing on these in difficult times helps you to stay strong, or using creativity helps you to get out of difficult situations, or strengths of organisation, judgement and being strategic help to create order and clarity.

I sit in the middle of this debate. I find it really helpful for leaders to enhance their strengths: I've seen many examples of where focusing energy on what you are already good at significantly improves impact and performance. However, there are some skills that I think need to be learnt. For example, for someone whose strengths are about achieving, judgement and being strategic, there may be an absence of strong relational skills. Learning the mechanics of conversations, about the ego states, knowing about threat and reward and who responds to what prompts, knowing about what causes resistance and how to avoid that when leading and influencing, are pretty useful skills to add to your repertoire. Learning these doesn't change who you are, they change how well you present your strengths and the impact these have on others.

17.6 I'm an introverted leader – does it matter?

Personality tests differentiate between extroverts and introverts, a paradigm I think is highly misunderstood. The dictionary definition of an extrovert is 'a socially outgoing person' and an introvert a 'shy reticent person'. I have a different, more psychological take, I think of these as preferences:

- An extrovert likes to think out loud, their ideas flow with an audience, they thrive around people and need high levels of social interaction
- An introvert prefers to do their thinking inside of their heads, needing quiet to do their best thinking. They need less, not no, social support and to self-manage and be resilient, they prefer time alone

There's also the ambivert position, which is somewhere in between, as these two are seen as a continuum. Extrovert leaders can overwhelm with their pressure of speech, they can be unintentionally misleading as, by thinking aloud, they are not providing clarity. They usually thrive in a high positive Stroke environment. Introverted leaders may not communicate enough for more outgoing colleagues, they often like fewer positive Strokes and therefore struggle with the positive Stroke needs others may thrive on. They find speaking up in group sessions harder. It's thought that current day leadership environments support extroverts and ambiverts best, as so much of leadership is relational.

However, the biggest advocate for introverted leaders, Susan Cain, argues in her book *Quiet* (2013) that introverts make great leaders as they are more likely to share power and give others the space to express ideas. They influence a more thoughtful, more balanced, less excitable culture. They can choose moments to be more gregarious, rather than this being 'on tap' and, when careful consideration is required, it is best to have an introvert to follow.

17.7 Self-leadership: self-awareness and habitual change – the beginning of leadership development

Everything I've talked about in this book requires self-awareness and self-management. The leadership programmes I run usually start with activities to increase self-awareness. There are whole leadership programmes these days referred to as 'self-leadership', which means understanding who you are and working consciously towards goals. Some leadership developers distinguish leadership, as influencing others, from self-leadership, as influencing and intentionally guiding oneself.

According to these definitions this has been a book on both self-leadership and leadership. I hope that you've found it a book that has helped you to be more self-aware, to know what sort of leader you are and want to be, what impact you have and, crucially, understand how to make changes to be both a more effective self-leader and a leader who influences others. It's not a book about changing yourself, it's about knowing yourself and adapting your leadership style, your mindset, managing your emotions and making different, even more effective. behavioural choices in order to lead better.

Changing your leadership style requires a set of intentional habit changes. In order to change a habit we need to do four actions. According to James Clear in *Atomic Habits* (2018), we need:

1. A desire for change: a good purpose for a change in habit, a good reason to think or to behave differently
2. A clear, easy trigger: an immediate reminder to use the new way
3. To make the response easy where it doesn't take up much of our precious time, where it's not complicated. One of the easiest methods is to add this adaptation to an existing routine
4. Built in rewards as satisfaction, dopamine, increases 'stickiness'

Good luck!

17.8 Self-reflection

- Why do you want to lead? Are you leading for the right reasons?
- What sort of leader do you aspire to be? Does that work for the people you lead and the culture in which you work?
- Can your leadership challenges be overcome through learning and experience? Or is it time to change your aspiration?
- Are you pumping too many resources into supporting someone (or yourself) who isn't a good leader? What's the alternative?
- Are you too hard on yourself? What can you do about this?
- Are you taking enough responsibility for your actions? Is there someone with whom you need to make reparation?
- Is it time for some coaching or mentoring?
- Do you lead through your strengths? What can you do to enhance your strengths?
- Are you an extrovert, an ambivert or an introvert? How does this impact your leadership?
- Can you identify a new effective leadership habit to start this week?

Note

1 See for example, Peterson and Seligman (2004).

References

Cain, S. (2013). *Quiet: The power of introverts in a world that can't stop talking.* Penguin.

Clear, J. (2018*). Atomic habits: The easy and proven way to build good habits and break bad ones.* Penguin.

Nichols, S. (2024, 30 July). *The future of leadership development.* [Webinar], SMRS. https://www.eventbrite.co.uk/e/webinar-future-of-leadership-development-tickets-91611 1262447

Owen, D., & Davidson, J. (2009). Hubris syndrome: An acquired personality disorder? A study of US Presidents and UK Prime Ministers over the last 100 years *Brain, 132*(5), 1396–1406. https://doi.org/10.1093/brain/awp008

Peterson, C., & Seligman, M. (2004). *Character strengths and virtues: A handbook and classification.* Oxford University Press.

Wageman, R. (2021, 9–10 May). Six conditions for team effectiveness: The science and art of great teams. Paper presented to the Psychological Society Special Group in Coaching Psychology Conference, 2021.

INDEX

For Product Safety Concerns and Information please contact our EU
representative GPSR@taylorandfrancis.com
Taylor & Francis Verlag GmbH, Kaufingerstraße 24, 80331 München, Germany

www.ingramcontent.com/pod-product-compliance
Lightning Source LLC
Chambersburg PA
CBHW070335270326
41926CB00017B/3880

* 9 7 8 1 0 4 1 0 3 3 1 0 3 *